This book may be kept

FOURTEEN DAYS

A fine of TWO CENTS will be charged for each day
the book is kept over time.

Mar 13'51			
Mar 15'54			

ADDRESSES

UPON

THE AMERICAN ROAD

1948–1950

ADDRESSES

UPON

THE AMERICAN ROAD

BY

Herbert Hoover

1948–1950

1951
STANFORD UNIVERSITY PRESS
STANFORD, CALIFORNIA

STANFORD UNIVERSITY PRESS
STANFORD, CALIFORNIA

London : Geoffrey Cumberlege
Oxford University Press

—

THE BAKER AND TAYLOR COMPANY
55 FIFTH AVENUE, NEW YORK 3

HENRY M. SNYDER & COMPANY
440 FOURTH AVENUE, NEW YORK 16

W. S. HALL & COMPANY
457 MADISON AVENUE, NEW YORK 22

—

Contents

v

vii

viii

ix

PART I

DOMESTIC POLICIES
AND ECONOMICS

The Miracle of America*

Woman's Home Companion
[November 1948]

URING the last score of years our American form of civilization has been deluged with criticism. It comes from our own people who deplore our undoubted faults and genuinely wish to remedy them. It comes from our political parties by their denunciations in debate of our current issues. It arises from the forthright refusal of the American people to wash their dirty linen in secret. It comes from our love of sensational incidents where villainy is pursued by law and virtue triumphs. It comes from intellectuals who believe in the American system but who feel that our moral and spiritual greatness has not risen to the level of our industrial accomplishments.

Criticism also comes from our native Communists who want to overturn the system. And from the fuzzy-minded totalitarian liberals who believe that their creeping collectivism can be adopted without destroying personal liberty and representative government. It comes bitterly and daily from the governments behind the Iron Curtain and their officials and even from the press of the western European nations that we are trying to help.

Altogether we seem to be in a very, very bad way and engaged in our decline and fall. Criticism is no doubt good for our national soul—if it does not discourage us entirely.

* Copyright 1948 by the Crowell-Collier Publishing Company.

3

Perhaps the time has come for Americans to take a little stock and think something good about themselves.

We could point out that our American system has perfected the greatest productivity of any nation on earth; that our standard of living is the highest in the world. We could point to our constantly improving physical health and lengthening span of life. We could mention the physical condition of our youth as indicated somewhat by our showing in the recent Olympic games.

In the governmental field, we could suggest that our supposedly decadent people still rely upon the miracle of the ballot and the legislative hall to settle their differences of view and not upon a secret police with slave camps.

In the cultural field, we could point out that with only about six per cent of the world's population we have more youth in high schools and institutions of higher learning, more musical and literary organizations, more libraries and probably more distribution of the printed and spoken word than all the other ninety-four per cent put together.

On the moral and spiritual side, we have more hospitals and charitable institutions than all of them. And we could suggest that we alone, of all nations, fought in two world wars and asked no indemnities, no acquisition of territory, no domination over other nations. We could point to an advancement of the spirit of Christian compassion such as the world has never seen, and prove it by the tons of food and clothes and billions of dollars we have made as gifts in saving hundreds of millions from famine and governments from collapse.

Much as I feel deeply the lag in spots which do not give equal chance to our Negro population, yet I cannot refrain from saying that our twelve million Negroes probably own more automobiles than all the two hundred million Russians or the three hundred million Negroes under European governments in Africa.

All of which is not boasting, but just fact. And we could say a good deal more.

Whatever our faults may be, our critics do not grasp the sense of a word which is daily on our lips—America. From its intangible meanings spring the multitude of actions, ideals and purposes of our people. Recently I had an occasion to say something on that subject which I can summarize here.

America means far more than a continent bounded by two oceans. It is more than pride of military power, glory in war or in victory. It means more than vast expanse of farms, of great factories or mines, magnificent cities or millions of automobiles and radios. It is more even than the traditions of the great tide westward from Europe which pioneered the conquest of a continent. It is more than our literature, our music, our poetry. Other nations have these things also.

What we have in addition, the intangible we cannot describe, lies in the personal experience and the living of each of us rather than in phrases, however inspiring.

Perhaps without immodesty I can claim to have had some experience in what *American* means. I have lived many kinds of American life. After my early boyhood in an Iowa village, I lived as the ward of a country doctor in Oregon. I lived among those to whom hard work was the price of existence. The opportunities of America opened up to me the public schools. They carried me to the professional training of an American university. I began by working with my own hands for my daily bread. I have tasted the despair of fruitless search for a job. I know the kindly encouragement of a humble boardinghouse keeper.

I have conducted the administration of great industries with their problems of production and the well-being of their employees.

I have seen America in contrast with many nations and races. My profession took me into many foreign lands under many kinds of government. I have worked with their great spiritual leaders and their great statesmen. I have worked in governments of free men, of tyrannies, of Socialists and of Communists. I have met with princes, kings, despots and desperadoes.

I have seen the squalor of Asia, the frozen class barriers of Europe. I was not a tourist. I was associated in their working lives and problems. I had to deal with their social systems and their governments. And outstanding everywhere to these great masses of people there was a hallowed word—*America*. To them it was the hope of the world.

Every homecoming was for me a reaffirmation of the glory of America. Each time my soul was washed by the relief from the grinding poverty of other nations, by the greater kindliness and frankness which comes from acceptance of equality and the wide-open opportunity to all who want a chance. It is more than that. It is a land of self-respect born alone of free men.

In later years I participated on behalf of America in a great war. I saw untold misery and revolution. I have seen liberty die and tyranny rise. I have seen human slavery again on the march.

I have been repeatedly placed by my countrymen where I had need to deal with the hurricanes of social and economic destruction which have swept the world. I have seen bitter famine and the worst misery that the brutality of war can produce.

I have had every honor to which any man could aspire. There is no place on the whole earth except here in America where all the sons of man could have this chance in life.

The meaning of our word *America* flows from one pure source. Within the soul of America is the freedom of mind and spirit in man. Here alone are the open windows through which pours the sunlight of the human spirit. Here alone human dignity is not a dream but a major accomplishment.

At the time our ancestors were proclaiming that the Creator had endowed all mankind with rights of freedom as the children of God, with a free will, the German philosophers, Hegel and others, and later Karl Marx, were proclaiming a satanic philosophy of agnosticism and that the rights of man came from the state. The greatness of America today comes from one philosophy, the despair of Europe from the other.

But there are people in our country today who would compromise in these fundamental concepts. They scoff at these tested qualities in men. They never have understood and never will understand what the word *America* means. They explain that these qualities were good while there was a continent to conquer and a nation to build. They say that time has passed.

No doubt the land frontier has passed. But the frontiers of science and better understanding of human welfare are barely opening.

This new land of science with all its high promise cannot and will not be conquered except by men and women inspired by these same concepts of free spirit and free mind.

And it is those moral and spiritual qualities which rise alone in free men which will fulfill the meaning of the word *American*. And with them will come centuries of further greatness to our country.

Give Us Self-Reliance —
or Give Us Security

Address at Ohio Wesleyan University,
Delaware, Ohio
[June 11, 1949]

I AM glad to come to Ohio Wesleyan University today to
take part in the formal installation of my friend Arthur
Flemming as your President. I know more about him than
I do about John Wesley. But every American knows Wesley
as the founder of a great movement which has inspired millions
to righteous living.

I am, however, concerned with Mr. Flemming. I need not
tell you that he is a son of this University, or of his years of
public service in war and peace.

I have worked with him intimately for the past two years.
He was better fitted for the work of the Commission on Organization of the Executive Branch of the Government than any of
the rest of us. He brought high statesmanship and great understanding of its human problems. I can condense the many things
I could say of Dr. Flemming into two short sentences:

President Flemming will be one of the great American university presidents. That is one of the highest positions of leadership in our American life.

This season you and a mighty host of 500,000 other American graduates are lining up to receive your college diplomas.

Once upon a time, I lined up just as you are. For me, it was
a day of lowered spirit. The night before we had omitted the
cheerful song about "The Owl and the Pussy Cat," and chanted

of "Working on the Railroad" and that immortal college dirge about going "Into the Cold, Cold World." The dynamic energy and the impelling desire to crack something up had sunk to low action levels.

I had to listen to an address made up of the standardized parts which were at that time generally sold at Commencements. It took over an hour for the speaker to put the parts together. We were warned that our diploma was an entrance ticket to jungles of temptation and hard knocks. Our speaker dwelled upon the Founding Fathers, the division of powers, upon Herbert Spencer and John Stuart Mill. He said we were living in a New Era in the world. He described it as Liberalism. The idea had to do with free minds and free spirits. It included the notion that America was a land of opportunity—with the great ideal of being a land of *equal* opportunity. We were told that life was a race where society laid down rules of sportsmanship but "let the best man win." The encouraging note in his address was emphasis upon Christian in *The Pilgrim's Progress* and Horatio Alger.

I confess my attention on that occasion was distracted by a sinking realization that I had to find a job—and quick. Also, I knew a girl. Put in economic terms, I was wishing somebody with a profit motive would allow me to help him earn a profit, and thus support the girl. At the risk of seeming revolutionary and a defender of evil, I suggest that this basis of test for a job has considerable merit. It does not require qualifications either of good looks, ancestry, religion, or ability to get votes.

It is true that I had some difficulty in impressing any of the profit and loss takers with the high potentialities of my diploma. But I was without the information at that time that I was a wage slave. I was buoyed up with the notion that if I did not like any particular profit taker, I could find another one somewhere else.

And let me add, that under that particular New Era I did not find a cold, cold world. I found the profit takers a cheery and helpful lot of folks, who took an enormous interest in helping youngsters get a start and get ahead in life. And you will find that is also true today. Indeed, their helpfulness has improved, for, as technology becomes more intricate, they are searching for skills, and your diploma commands more respect.

And now voices tell us that we are in another New Era. In fact, we seem to have a newer era every little while.

Incidentally, I entered the cold, cold world in the midst of what the latest New Era calls a "disinflation." We mistakenly thought its name was "depression." But as I did not then know that governments could cure it, I did not have the additional worry of what the Government was going to do about it.

The new era of today seems united in the notion that they have just discovered real Liberalism and that all previous eras are reactionary. Some tell us that, in their New Era, life is still a race, but that everybody must come out even at the end. Another modernistic school adds to this that life still may be a race, but that each step must be dictated by some official or unofficial bureaucrat with Stop-and-Go signals. They hold out the attraction that with this security you will finish with an old-age pension and your funeral expenses from the Government.

Whether these newest eras are right or wrong, "security," which eliminates the risks in life, also kills the joy that lies in competition, in individual adventure, new undertakings, and new achievements. These contain moral and intellectual impulses more vital than even profits. For from them alone comes national progress. At all times in history there have been many who sought escape into "security" from self-reliance.

And if you will look over the workings of these newest New Eras throughout the world, you may notice that the judgment of the Lord on Adam has not been entirely reversed, even by the Supreme Court of the United States. Moreover, governments have not been able to fix the wages of sin. Nor have they found a substitute for profit and other personal stimulants.

America has not yet embraced all these new ideas. The reactionary notion of equal opportunity with the right of everyone to go as far as his ambitions and abilities will take him, provided he does not trespass on others, still holds in the American dream.

How far he can get has been damaged by two great wars and

inefficiently organized government, which we have to pay for. To pay it, you will need to work two days out of the week for the Government for a long time. The Commission upon which President Flemming and I have taken part is trying to take a few hours off that penalty.

And there is something more to be said for the old reactionary notions which held to basic freedoms of mind and spirit, holding aloft the lamp of equal opportunity. In the years since the Founding Fathers, a God-fearing people, under these reactionary blessings, built up quite a plant and equipment on this continent. It teems with millions of comfortable farms and homes, cattle and hogs. It is well equipped with railroads, power plants, factories, highways, automobiles and death warnings. It is studded with magnificent cities and traffic jams. The terrible reactionaries have filled the land with legislatures, town councils, free presses, orchestras, bands, radios, juke-boxes and other noises. It has a full complement of stadiums, ball players and college yells. Furthermore, they sprinkled the country with churches and laboratories, built ten thousand schools and a thousand institutions of higher learning. And somehow, these reactionary-minded taxpayers are squeezing out the resources to maintain a million devoted teachers, a hundred thousand able professors, and to keep over two million of you in colleges and universities. Possibly, another ideology could do better in the next one hundred and seventy-three years. But I suggest we had better continue to suffer certain evils of free men and the ideal of equal opportunity than to die of nostalgia.

It is very sad, but did it ever occur to you that all the people who live in these houses and all those who run this complicated machine are going to die? Just as sure as death, the jobs are yours. The plant and equipment comes to you by inheritance ready to run. And there are opportunities in every inch of it. But the best of these jobs are never filled by security seekers.

Moreover, there are other vast opportunities for those who are willing to take a chance. If we just hold to our reactionary ideas of free minds, free spirits, and equal opportunity, we have another glorious opening for every young man and woman. Science and invention, even during these troubled years, have given us further mighty powers of progress. New discoveries in science and their flow of new inventions will continue to create a thousand new frontiers for those who still would adventure.

You have the blood and the urge of your American forebears. You are made of as good stuff as they. I have no doubt of your character and your self-reliance. You are better trained and equipped than we were. I know you are champing at the bit to take your chance in an opening world.

Do not fear it will be cold to you.

Think of the Next Generation

*Birthday Address at the Reception
Tendered by Stanford University
[August 10, 1949]*

M Y FIRST duty is to acknowledge your generous reception. And I wish at once to express my gratitude for the many thousands of messages I have received from officials and citizens both from at home and abroad.

I wish also to express my gratitude for the wonderful support that has come to the Library. That is a surprise and will serve a great purpose.

It is now thirty-four years since this Institute and Library was founded. Over these years friends of the Library have contributed great sums toward its support. And of priceless value have been the millions of documents and materials furnished freely by hundreds of individuals and three-score governments.

This institution is not a dead storage. It is a living thing. Here thousands of students and, during the war, military officers, have been trained for international service. Over the future years research in these shelves will correct a vast amount of error in the history of these troubled times. It will also teach the stern lessons of how nations may avoid war and revolution.

On this occasion it would be a great pleasure to discuss the problems and the immense gains our nation is making from the training of the host of 2,500,000 young men and women now in our institutions of higher learning.

Such a host is unprecedented in all the history of mankind. To this work this University is doing its full part.

But in the sombre situation of the world I have felt that I should discuss another subject which weighs heavy on my heart, for it involves the future of all these young men and women.

Some of you will know that during the past two years I have added somewhat to my previous knowledge of the currents of government in this Republic. Beyond the immediate problems of efficient organization of the Federal Departments, there arise from these investigations some grave questions relating to the next generation and indeed to our whole future as a nation.

THE NEED FOR SOME THINKING

Now, as never before, we need thinking on some of these questions. If America is to be run by the people, it is the people who must think, and think now. And we do not need to put on sackcloth and ashes to think. Nor should our minds work like a sundial which records only sunshine. However, our thinking must square against some lessons of history, some principles of government and morals, if we would preserve the rights and dignity of men to which this nation is dedicated.

The real test of our thinking is not so much the next election as it is the next generation.

I am not going to offer you solutions to our national ills. But I shall list some items for thought. Perhaps in Japanese-English a subhead would be "Bring feet from clouds into swamp where we now are."

THE GROWTH OF GOVERNMENTAL SPENDING

We must wish to maintain a dynamic progressive people. No nation can remain static and survive. But dynamic progress is not made with dynamite. And that dynamite today is the geometrical increase of spending by our governments—Federal, state, municipal and local.

Perhaps I can visualize what this growth has been. Twenty years ago, all varieties of government, omitting Federal debt service, cost the average family less than $200 annually. Today, also omitting debt service, it costs an average family about $1,300 annually.

This is bad enough. But beyond this is the alarming fact that at this moment executives and legislatures are seriously proposing projects which if enacted would add one-third more annually to our spending. Add to these the debt service and the average family may be paying $1,900 yearly taxes. They may get a little back if they live to over 65 years of age.

It does not seem very generous to set up an "acceptable" standard of living and then make it impossible by taxes.

THE GROWTH OF BUREAUCRACY

No doubt life was simpler about 147 years ago, when our government got well under way. At that time there was less than one government employee, Federal, state and local including the paid military, to each 120 of the population. Twenty years ago, there was one government employee to about 40 of the population. Today, there is one government employee to about every 22 of the population. Worse than this, there is today one government employee to about 8 of the working population in the United States.

THE GROWTH OF DEPENDENCY

Twenty years ago, persons directly or indirectly receiving regular monies from the government—that is, officials, soldiers, sailors, pensioners, subsidized persons and contractors' employees working exclusively for the government—represented about one person in every 40 of the population.

Today a little more than one person out of every 7 in the population is a regular recipient of government monies. If those of age are all married, they comprise about one-half the voters of the last Presidential election.

Think it over.

WORKING FOR THE GOVERNMENT

In the long run it is the Average Working Citizen who pays by hidden and other taxes. I have made up a little table showing the number of days which this kind of citizen must work on average to pay the taxes.

	Days' Work
Obligations from former wars	11
Defense and Cold War	24
Other federal expenditures	12
State and local expenditures	14
Total thus far	61

But beyond this the seriously proposed further spending now in process will take another 20 days' work from Mr. and Mrs. Average W. Citizen.

Taking out holidays, Sundays, and average vacations, there are about 235 working days in the year. Therefore, this total of 81 days' work a year for taxes will be about one week out of every month.

You might want to work for your family instead of paying for a gigantic bureaucracy.

Think it over.

CONFISCATION OF SAVINGS

To examine what we are doing, we must get away from such sunshine figures as the gross national income. We must reduce our problem to the possible savings of the people after a desirable standard of living. If we adopt the Federal Government's estimate of such a desirable standard, then the actual, and the seriously proposed, national and local government spending will absorb between 75 percent to 85 percent of all the savings of the people. In practice it does not work evenly. The few will have some savings, but the many must reduce their standard of living below the "acceptable" level to pay the tax collector.

And it is out of savings that the people must provide their individual and family security. From savings they must buy their homes, their farms, and their insurance. It is from their savings finding their way into investment that we sustain and stimulate progress in a dynamic productive system.

One end result of the actual and proposed spendings and taxes to meet them is that the Government becomes the major source of credit and capital to the economic system. At best the small business man is starved in the capital he can find. Venture capital to develop new ideas tends to become confined to the large corporations and they grow bigger. There are ample signs of these results already.

Governments do not develop gadgets of improved living.

Another end result is to expose all our independent colleges and other privately supported institutions to the risk of becoming dependent upon the state. Already it is more and more difficult for these institutions to find resources.

Then through politics we will undermine their independence which gives lifting standards and stimulus to government supported institutions.

No nation grows stronger by such subtraction.

Think it over.

GOVERNMENT BORROWING

It is proposed that we can avoid these disasters by more government borrowing. That is a device to load our extravagance and waste on to the next generation. But increasing government debts can carry immediate punishment for that is the road to inflation. There is far more courage in reducing our gigantic national debt than in increasing it. And that is a duty to our children.

INCREASING TAXES

And there is no room for this spending and taxes except to cut the standard of living of most of our people below the "ac-

ceptable" level. It is easy to say, "Increase corporation taxes."
That is an illusion. The bulk of corporation taxes is passed on
to the consumer—that is, to every family. It is easy to say, "Increase taxes on the higher personal income brackets." But if all
incomes over $8,000 a year were confiscated, it would cover less
than 10 percent of these actual and proposed spendings.

The real road before us is to reduce spending and waste and
defer some desirable things for a while.

WE CANNOT HAVE EVERYTHING AT ONCE

There are many absolute necessities and there are many less
urgent meritorious and desirable things that every individual
family in the nation would like to have but cannot afford. To
spend for them, or borrow money for them, would endanger the
family home and the family life. So it is with the national
family.

So long as we must support the necessary national defense
and cold war at a cost of 24 days' work per year to Mr. Average
W. Citizen there are many comforting things that should be deferred if we do not wish to continue on this road to ruin of our
national family life.

Think it over.

THE BACK ROAD TO COLLECTIVISM

The American mind is troubled by the growth of collectivism
throughout the world.

We have a few hundred thousand Communists and their fellow travelers in this country. They cannot destroy the Republic.
They are a nuisance and require attention. We also have the doc-
trinaire socialists who peacefully dream of their utopia.

But there is a considerable group of fuzzy-minded people
who are engineering a compromise between free men and these
European infections. They fail to realize that our American
system has grown away from the systems of Europe for 250
years. They have the foolish notion that a collectivist economy

can at the same time preserve personal liberty and constitutional government. That cannot be done.

The steady lowering of the standard of living by this compromised collectivist system under the title "austerity" in England should be a sufficient spectacle for the American people. It aims at an abundant life but it ends in a ration.

Most Americans do not believe in these compromises with collectivism. But they do not realize that through governmental spending and taxes, our nation is blissfully driving down the back road to it at top speed.

In the end these solutions of national problems by spending are always the same—power, more power, more centralization in the hands of the state.

Along this road of spending, the Government either takes over economic life, which is socialism, or dictates institutional and economic life, which is fascism.

We have not had a great socialization of property, but we are on the last miles to collectivism through governmental spending of the savings of the people.

Think it over.

FOOLING THE PEOPLE'S THINKING

A device of these advocates of gigantic spending is the manipulation of words, phrases, and slogans to convey new meanings different from those we have long understood. These malign distortions drug thinking. They drown it in emotion.

For instance, we see government borrowing and spending transformed into the soft phrase "deficit spending." The slogan of a "welfare state" has emerged as a disguise for a collectivist state by the route of spending. The Founding Fathers would not recognize this distortion of the simple word "welfare" in the Constitution. Certainly Jefferson's idea of the meaning of welfare lies in his statement "To preserve our independence . . . . we must make a choice between economy and liberty or profusion and servitude. . . . . If we can prevent government from wresting the labors of the people under the pretence of caring for them we shall be happy."

Another of these distortions is by those who support such a
state and call themselves "liberals." John Morley would not
recognize one of them.

Out of these slogans and phrases and new meanings of words
come vague promises and misty mirages, such as "security from
the cradle to the grave." In action that will frustrate those basic
human impulses to production which alone make a dynamic nation.

Think it over.

WHERE BLAME MUST BE PLACED

It is customary to blame our Administrations or our legislatures for this gigantic increase in spending, these levies on the
nation's workdays, and this ride to a dead-end of our unique and
successful American system. A large cause of this growing con-
fiscation of the work of the people by our various governments
is the multitude of great pressure groups among our own citizens.
Also the state and municipal governments pressurize the Federal Government. And within the Federal Government are
pressure groups building their own empires.

Aggression of groups and agencies against the savings of the
people as a whole is not a process of free men. Special privilege
either to business or groups is not liberty.

Many of these groups maintain paid lobbies in Washington
or in the State Capitols to press their claims upon the Administrations or the legislatures.

Our representatives must run for election. They can be defeated by these pressure groups. In any event our officials are
forced to think in terms of pressure groups, not in terms of need
of the whole people.

Perhaps some of my listeners object to somebody else's pressure group. Perhaps you support one of your own. Perhaps
some of you do not protest that your leaders are not acting with
your authority.

Think it over.

IN CONCLUSION

And finally, may I say that thinking and debate on these questions must not be limited to legislative halls. We should debate them in every school. We should resort to the old cracker barrel debate in every corner grocery. In those places these phrases and slogans can be liquidated by common sense and intellectual integrity.

A splendid storehouse of integrity and freedom has been bequeathed to us by our forefathers. In this day of confusion, of world peril to free men, our high duty is to see that this storehouse is not robbed of its contents.

We dare not see the birthright of posterity to individual independence, initiative and freedom of choice bartered for a mess of collectivism.

My word to you, my fellow-citizens, on this seventy-fifth birthday is this: The Founding Fathers dedicated the structure of our government "to secure the blessings of liberty to ourselves and our posterity." A century and a half later, we of this generation still inherited this precious blessing. Yet as spendthrifts we are on our way to rob posterity of its inheritance.

The American people have solved many great difficulties in the development of national life. The qualities of self-restraint, of integrity, of conscience and courage still live in our people. It is not too late to summon these qualities into action.

Debts, Deficits, and Taxes

*Address before the United States Junior Chamber
of Commerce, Chicago, Illinois
[June 16, 1950]*

IT IS a pleasure to address the Junior Chamber of Commerce. We owe to you a debt for the support you have given to reorganizing the executive machinery of the Government. There are even more reasons for public appreciation of your organization which I will mention later.

Some of your officers asked me to speak on the relation of Government expenditures, deficits, and taxes, to jobs and to national life.

THE FIVE QUESTIONS

They propounded to me five questions:

1. Who pays these taxes?
2. Can taxes be sufficiently increased to meet these deficits?
3. Will deficits not lead to more inflation?
4. Can expenses be reduced?
5. What stands in the way of reductions?

It is these five questions, plus the activities of the different breeds of collectivists, which plague the American people today.

Before I attempt to answer these questions, I will make a few preparatory observations.

Today we are blessed with some kind of prosperity. Whatever kind it is, we all want stability without inflation. We want a system that finds jobs for 1,000,000 new workers each year.

DEFICITS IN GENERAL

In 1932 I did the suffering from an unbalanced budget. The reverberations of a European panic had pulled the tax revenues out from under us, and we were compelled to make large recoverable loans to support our credit structure. Outside these subsequently recovered loans our modest deficit was about $1 billion. In the midst of this grief, Mr. Roosevelt, in denouncing our deficit, made an uncomfortable remark to the effect that, too often, liberal governments have been wrecked on the rock of deficits. However, we only heard this remark once.

About this time, Lord John Maynard Keynes came up with his new intoxicant of deficit spending in years of unemployment. It had a good political flavor. Having got the habit, we keep drinking in times of presumed prosperity. With the exception of two years in the 80th Congress, we have had deficits and increasing debt for all 17 years since Keynes helped us out.

The consoling answer of the inebriated is that there is really no such thing as Government debt. They say, "We owe it to ourselves." Any government which follows this will-o'-the-wisp will sometime break its neck over the precipice of inflation. Some have already done so.

DEFICITS IN PROSPECT

We cannot appraise these questions without using facts, figures and the word billions. But, to be sure the billions I mention are free of political bias, I use only those from Democratic Senators.

Senator Harry Byrd says that if we include all Federal expenditures, both in and outside of the President's formal budget, they will amount to about $44 billions for the present fiscal year, with a deficit of about $5 billions. Our State and local expenditures amount to about $15 billions. That would be around $60 billions of various current Government expenditures.

Beyond this Senator McClellan calculates that, if all the recommended Federal legislation is passed, it will increase the annual Federal expenditures by $20 to $25 billions more. Senator McClellan is against this phantasmagoria of the Promised Land which he so well appraised. Even without this phantasmagoria, the Federal deficit will probably be greater next year, and there are also powerful urgings to state and municipal governments for increased expenditures.

WHO PAYS THE TAXES?

The first of your questions was, "Who pays the taxes?" Here we enter a land of twilights and illusions. We can illuminate it somewhat if we divide the taxpayers into the sheep and the goats. The sheep are the families who have a gross income of less than $7,000 a year before taxes. The goats are those who have a gross income of more than $7,000 a year. Various studies show that almost 80 percent of Governmental revenues come from the sheep. It also shows that each sheep family on the average pays about $1,400 a year in taxes and deductions. Therefore even the $7,000 top figure for the sheep is not $7,000. Your second question was:

CAN TAXES BE INCREASED TO MEET THESE DEFICITS?

I suppose taxes could be increased until the whole population can no longer buy enough food or clothes. The real question is how far our people can be taxed and still have jobs and a decent standard of living. We can apply four tests as to whether the patient can stand any more tax mixtures.

First. Because of the average $1,400 annual taxes on the sheep families, a large number of them are already prevented from reaching the standard which the Labor Department insists is "desirable."

Second. But how about the goats who have gross incomes of more than $7,000 a year? The answer is easy. If the Government confiscated their *entire* personal incomes, it would not pay the present Federal deficit—and that does not include Senator McClellan's phantasmagoria of a Promised Land.

Third. One of the illusions of our times is that corporation taxes come from the stockholders. Sometime the American people will realize that corporation taxes are passed on to the customers, which are the sheep. Otherwise the corporations would in the end go bankrupt.

Therefore, any substantial increase in taxes must come by shearing more from the sheep.

Fourth. It is my belief that even present taxes are so draining the savings of the people into the Government as to undermine new jobs for the future. It is possible to calculate the present Government take as theoretically over 60 percent of the people's savings after deducting the cost of a possible decent standard of living. If the phantasmagoria described by Senator McClellan came into action, the Government take would be over 80 percent.

The fact that taxes have already definitely shrunken venture and equity capital for small business would seem to be proved when the Government proposes to furnish such capital. Never before, in 165 years, did small business depend on Government. Small businesses are the plants from which big business grows.

That is also proof that the Government is becoming more and more the source of capital and credit. To which the socialists applaud.

Big business can finance itself by borrowing money, especially while the Government is inflating credit. But big business only employs about 25 percent of the working population.

The answer to the question, "Can our economy stand substantially more taxes and still make substantial progress?" is just simply NO, unless you believe a collectivist state is progress. Your third question was:

WILL DEFICITS LEAD TO MORE INFLATION?

Financing Government deficits by borrowing, if continued long enough, has only one end—Inflation. That has been proved by a dozen nations.

We ourselves have already decreased the purchasing value

of the dollar by over 40 percent and we are still creeping along that road. The five-cent telephone call went a few weeks ago and the five-cent fare had already gone, and the five-cent candy bar has shrunk even more lately. A new round of inflation is now appearing in direct or indirect wage and salary increases and rising commodity prices.

If we keep on this road, we are certain to reach the President's ideal of $4,000 a year to every family. But it will not have $4,000 purchasing power.

To this question of further Government borrowing to meet deficits, my answer is that it is the road to disaster for every cottage in the land. Your fourth question was:

CAN WE REDUCE EXPENSES?

To that, the answer is YES.

The first move in that direction is to stop the phantasmagoria described by Senator McClellan in its tracks. That is easy if we take a holiday in new Government services until the deficit is overcome. No doubt many things the Government can provide are desirable. Most every family would like to add desirable things to its living. But getting them by borrowing money is the way the old homestead was lost. Most families shy off that method. And the Government should be even more shy, or it will come to a bad end.

The second and most simple device to reduce expenses is for Congress to cut proposed expenditures to the very bones of necessity; also to suspend the sports of log-rolling and pork barrels.

We are generally told that these enormous Government expenditures and deficits are mainly the inheritances of the war and cannot be helped. It is true that of the present budget of $44 billions, about $32 billions go to pay interest on the debt, veterans, national defense and subsidies to other countries to keep them comfortable in the cold war. Those items have been increased by only 15 percent in the last three years.

To get some look at expenditures not created by the wars, and to avoid any partisan flavor, we may start from a Democratic fiscal year of 17 years ago. This non-war part of the Government has increased expenditures 400 percent in 17 years and 50 percent in the last three years. No amount of claims that the purchasing value of the dollar has decreased or that the population has increased can explain these increases.

REORGANIZATION OF THE EXECUTIVE BRANCH

The third way to reduce expenses is the more efficient organization and the cutting out of waste in government on the lines proposed by the Reorganization Commission.

Through the co-operation of the Administration, the Congress, the Citizens' Committee and such organizations as yours, we have already made substantial progress in these reforms of the Executive Branch of the Government.

The major accomplishments are:

Unification of the Armed Forces;

Reorganization of the State Department;

Unification of the General Services;

Reorganization of the Government Merchant Marine.

They represent big money. In addition, a number of minor reforms have been accepted.

MAJOR REFORMS STILL TO DO

We still have many major reforms to accomplish. They include our proposals:

To reorganize the whole Civil Service into an honest-to-goodness career service based on merit with justice and encouragement in promotion. The experienced chairman of our task force unhesitatingly stated we could save 10 percent of the Federal payroll. That would be a little item of $600,000,000.

To put the Budgeting and Accounting of the Government on a business basis. There would be many savings possible if the Government could see itself in the mirror of an adequate accounting system.

To organize the Post Office into a modern business concern,

with management free from politics. With this reform and some increase in rates to special commercial users, I believe its deficit of half a billion could be overcome.

To reorganize the structure of the departments of Treasury, Agriculture, Commerce, Labor, Interior, and Housing so that each of them has, cheek by jowl, the agencies devoted to a related major purpose. That would fix responsibility for policies, create checks and balances, eliminate overlaps, competition and waste inevitable in activities now scattered all over the Government. The chairman of only one of those task forces said that $300,000,000 could be saved by that one unification.

To unify the Government Hospital Services so as to save $4- or $500,000,000 of unnecessary construction now authorized; at the same time to provide better medical service and better preparedness for war.

And there are scores of other reforms which are pointed at greater efficiency for less money.

These recommendations were founded upon two years of study by 18 task forces comprised of independent leading men and women of experience whose reports, recommendations and reasons are open to everybody.

These reforms are in the lap of the gods in Washington and the pressure groups at home.

WHAT STANDS IN THE WAY OF REDUCTION OF EXPENDITURES?

The next question is, "What stands in the way of these reforms and reductions?"

Over 25 years ago, I served on a Commission of Reorganization of the Executive Branch. I saw those reforms go to their burial with the following remarks:

" . . . Practically every single item has met with opposition from some vested official, or it has disturbed some vested habit, and offended some organized minority. It has aroused the paid propagandists. All of them are in favor of every item of reorganization except that which affects the activity in which they are specially interested. In the aggregate, these directors of vested habits and propaganda surround Congress with a confusing fog of opposition. Meantime, the inchoate voice of the public gets nowhere but to swear."

Here ended that funeral sermon of 25 years ago.

But we are doing better this time than 25 years ago, as we had little public or Congressional support at that time.

Among our public supporters, the Junior Chamber of Commerce has given its fine energies to educating the misguided lay members of obstructing pressure groups, and yours is a splendid, intelligent appreciation of what economy in government means.

I may take a parable from Dr. Flemming. A Boy Scout Master was calling the roll of his troop as to what good deed each had performed during the week. All passed except four. The Scout Master told the four to go at once and come back in the afternoon, each with a good deed to report. When they returned, the first replied that he had helped a lady across the street. The second, third and fourth made the same reply. The suspicious Scout Master inquired if this was all about the same lady. The first boy replied, "Yes, sir. She was on the wrong side of the road. It took all four of us to get her over."

PROBLEMS DEEPER THAN REORGANIZATION

But the problems which face us in fiscal questions are deeper in American life than reorganization of the executive departments.

We need to make an appraisal of some of the forces which produce these dangers from expenditures, deficits, inflation and drainage of savings into the Government.

It is possible to denounce public officials for all these dangers and ills. But do not overlook the fact that public officials get elected because they satisfy their constituents. Among their constituencies are the special groups who want something from the Treasury. Many of them are on guard to protect their members from losing established privilege. They all wear the clothing of public interest. They are active in electing their man while the other citizen sleeps.

We bitterly fought special privilege in business. This idea of special privilege in groups is a more modern development.

There are probably 200,000 voluntary associations in the United States of some kind or another, most of which give voice for or against something of public importance. Except for the collectivists, they are one of the essential foundation piers under the American system of life. They perform millions of services in developing public understanding and public action. They also serve the country by neutralizing each other before the Congressional committees.

The number of associations interested in increasing or preventing the decrease in Government expenditures is very small, probably not 50 of much consequence, but they are a powerful minority.

Nor do all these pressures come from the voluntary associations. The municipalities press the State governments and the State governments press the Federal government.

If such an unexpected thing were to happen as all these groups keeping their hands off expenditure questions and these reforms in government for twelve months, both in Washington and in the election districts, the Congress would do a great job not only in decreasing expenses but in the common interest of the nation.

MORALS AS WELL AS ECONOMICS

There is something else involved in all this problem.

Out of the war, as from all wars, the nation has had a spell of moral and spiritual sickness. It has been a period of great cynicism. With the lowered moral resistance of this period, unfair burdens have been placed on the people by particular groups. Too frequently do we hear a repetition of the excuse, "They got theirs; we will get ours," or Ben Franklin's remark about "God helps those who help themselves."

But if Ben were alive today he would say, "Free men were not created by drives of pressure groups on the public treasury."

CONCLUSION

Nations must inevitably suffer from their mistakes. But their survival depends upon their will, their courage, and their moral and spiritual fibre. If these qualities live, then unbalanced budgets and ideological disputes can be but a passing froth on the surface. The rise of American civilization was out of a people of such qualities. It has been sick but it is not in its decline and fall. All around us we see signs of moral and spiritual strength in the oncoming youth.

There is a difficult word I could use here—atavism—that is, the latent qualities which we inherit from our ancestors. They are coming back. Your organization is one of their expressions. In your leadership of American youth lies the hope and confidence of our country and of my generation.

On Proposed Social Security Legislation

Letter to the Honorable Robert L. Doughton,
Chairman, Ways and Means Committee,
House of Representatives,
Washington, D.C.
[April 25, 1949]

New York City
April 25, 1949

The Honorable Robert L. Doughton
Chairman of the Ways and Means Committee
House of Representatives
Washington, D.C.

Dear Mr. Congressman:

I beg to acknowledge your request that I make some comment on H.R. 2893 and H.R. 2892 which relate to revision and expansion of Federal Old-Age and Survivors' Insurance and the Federal-State public assistance programs.

The following notes relating to the systems existing at present are based upon data collected by the Commission on Organization of the Executive Branch. That Commission did not deal with policy questions to be determined by Congress. The views on policy expressed herein, therefore, are solely my own.

I wish to say at once that I strongly favor governmental provision for protection of the aged and their dependents.

The problem before the nation is to obtain a workable system, with a minimum of administrative cost, a minimum of bureaucracy, adjusted to the economic strength of the country which gives an assurance of security to this group. In my view, we have not yet found that system.

I should like to make two general observations:

1. There is an illusion about the whole Federal Old-Age and Survivors' Insurance. Because the taxes on payrolls are paid into a trust fund and paid out without appropriation by Congress, there is an idea that these are neither taxes nor Federal expenditures. They are both. They are just as much a burden upon our national economy as any other tax or any other Government expenditure. Also, payroll taxes, however justifiable, are, like all other taxes, a burden on the standard of living of the whole nation. A considerable part of the payroll taxes paid by employers in the long run is passed to the people as a whole in prices, and a considerable part of the taxes paid by wage earners is passed on by demands for increased wages.

2. There are many desirable things that every American home would like to have, but its income compels it to deny itself, at least temporarily. It is similar with the nation.

Since this legislation was originally passed in 1935, we have increased the total burden of Federal expenditures from about $9.7 billions a year to a prospective $45 billions a year, included in which are about $23 billions for defense and European aid— most of which constitutes the cost of the cold war.

Already our economy is up to the limit of endurance under this load. I believe we should go slow and hold further additions to this burden to the absolute minimum. When the cold war is over, we can afford many more domestic improvements.

I can find no satisfactory estimates of the cost of these two proposals if enacted into law. There would be, however, a huge increase in the tax burden on our economy from this legislation. I make some tentative estimates later on.

THE PRESENT SYSTEM

1. The old-age problem has been thrust upon the Federal Government largely by the great increase in longevity. Its dimensions are indicated by the fact that there will be by 1950

about 11,000,000 persons over 65 years of age. They will increase in numbers absolutely and relatively, both with the increase in population and with the constantly advancing protection to health.

2. The nation today is undertaking to solve the problem from three different directions:

First is the joint Federal-State assistance to which I shall refer as "State Systems." Forty-eight of the States and three other jurisdictions, with Federal aid, give old-age assistance, dependency, children's benefits, and other social services, based upon individual needs. The variations in the "needs" requirement are considerable, and in a few States are so liberally interpreted as to be practically universal old-age pensions. The total number of persons given assistance by the "State Systems" is about 2,300,000.

The average amount of payments to the aged in need in all 48 States is $42.02 per month per person. In the 46 most typical States based on need, the average payment is about $39.50 per month per person. These monthly payments vary greatly among the States—ranging from a low of about $20.00 to a high of about $78.00 a month in one State. The annual cost averages about $1,200,000,000—about one-half of which is paid by the States and about one-half by the Federal Government.

Second is the Federal Old-Age and Survivors' Insurance, based upon payroll taxes, to which I shall refer as the "Federal Insurance System." Benefits are now being paid out to about 2,260,000 persons at an annual cost of about $556,000,000, and averaging about $25.00 per person per month, including their dependents. The payments being insufficient for the needy, many must be supplemented by the "State Systems."

Third is a multitude of old-age pension and retirement systems in the country to which I shall refer as the "Independent Systems." They are in the main Federal veteran and military pensions and disability systems of this group which extend into the 65-year age group; Federal Civil Service retirement systems; the Railroad Retirement System; the old-age or retirement systems of the States and local governments; the old-age or retirement systems of universities, hospitals, fraternal organizations and other benevolent institutions, insurance companies, businesses and industries. There is now a new form of old-age and retirement system emerging in particular industries as the result of collective bargaining. These systems, together with pensions to veterans, bid fair to be further extended.

The number of persons now receiving pensions or aid from these "independent" services is estimated at about 2,300,000. The monthly payments under these systems are much higher, on the average, than the other two systems.

Theoretically, there are about 7,000,000 persons now receiving benefits from all three systems. This, however, includes dependents less than 65 years old and there are duplications because in many cases the benefits from the "Federal Insurance System" are inadequate and must be supplemented by the "State Systems."

FAULTS IN THE PRESENT "FEDERAL INSURANCE SYSTEM"

3. There are serious faults in the "Federal Insurance System."

a) The original concepts, as embodied in the Social Security Act of 1935, were that the money to pay for the benefits would come from employees and employers by a tax on payrolls, and that the system would be self-sustaining. The original actuarial basis of the system was faulty and was made worse by the legislation of 1939.

One of the methods of this system contemplated building up a reserve fund in the early years to compensate the subsequent increased benefits. The monies collected from the payrolls have been, and are at present, in excess of the payments to beneficiaries, and the trust fund of about $10 billions has been accumulated and invested in Government bonds. The growth of expenditures for benefits under the present act apparently will exhaust this reserve in from 5 to 10 years, and the general taxpayer will be forced to make up the annual deficit. This deficit, it is estimated, will rise ultimately to about $1.7 billions per annum.

b) An additional burden, however, is thrust on the general taxpayer. Under the present system the Federal Government has used the surplus income of the trust fund (amounting to the $10 billions) for its current expenses and placed its IOU (in the shape of Government bonds) in the trust fund for the money thus used. It is estimated that the benefits paid out will begin to exceed the receipts (upon the present basis of the payroll tax and benefits) in a few years. When this occurs, the Government must redeem its IOU's from the trust fund. The money to redeem them must come from the general taxpayer. Even if the bonds were sold to the public, ultimately they must be redeemed by the taxpayer. As those who have already paid the payroll deductions are also taxpayers, they will, to some extent, be paying for their insurance twice over.

I cannot agree with the economic arguments before your Committee which are to the contrary. The simple fact is that the money has been raised by a tax, and, except for benefits already paid, has been used as current expenditures by the Government, and must be replaced from somewhere—the taxpayer.

THE PROPOSED NEW LEGISLATION

4. I do not have the technical staff to analyze in detail the effect of the amendments to previous legislation implied in these two bills (H.R. 2893 and 2892). However, I make some overall observations which may be worthy of consideration by your Committee.

a) I suggest that the Committee consider abandoning the whole reserve fund concept and that the "Federal Insurance System" be put on a pay-as-you-go basis. It should be no more difficult to calculate for a year ahead the amount of payroll taxes required to meet the outgo than any other taxes. The present reserve fund of $10 billions could remain as a balance wheel. It could be drawn upon temporarily when advance calculations of the tax prove inadequate and then could be restored the following year. This procedure would enable the Congress to fix the tax as needed and to appropriate the budget annually. In the latter matter, it has no voice at all at present. Such a method of pay-and-collect-as-you-go would avoid the faults pointed out in the paragraphs 3 *a* and *b* (above).

I am aware it will be contended that this course would deprive the scheme of its purported actuarial basis. As a matter of fact, it has been abandoned under the present system. But more important, the basic fault of double payment by beneficiaries (3 *b* above) destroys all such actuarial contentions anyway. And the same situation will apply to the new legislation as it again proposes to increase reserves, and spend the increased money for current expenses of the Government, with ultimate replacement by the taxpayer.

b) To visualize what the plans under H.R. 2893 and 2892 mean, it is necessary to reduce them to some sort of figures. It is proposed in H.R. 2893 ("Federal Insurance System") to increase the taxes on payrolls, which now amount to about $1,700,-000,000 per annum, to about $4,800,000,000. Obviously, this is an increase in tax burdens by about $3,100,000,000 per annum at once.

As I have said, I can find no adequate estimates of the annual expenditures under these two bills. Some estimates of the costs of adopting H.R. 2893 ("Federal Insurance System") are given, but apparently they do not include all of the features in the bill. I have found no estimates of the cost of the additional grants-in-aid to the "State Systems" under H.R. 2892, or of the other direct expenditures implied in that bill. They are, apparently, large.

The estimated "Federal Insurance System" expenditures under H.R. 2893 alone are:

(Present expenditures	$ 556,000,000)
1950	1,750,000,000
1955	3,400,000,000
1960	5,900,000,000

(These figures as to H.R. 2893 are about half-way between the "high" and "low" estimates furnished to the Committee.)

The very large increase in Federal expenditures is obvious. Moreover, it is also obvious that the reserve fund, in the next ten years, would be greatly increased. This surplus of payroll taxes over the benefits paid out again is to be represented by more bonds and used for current expenses—and ultimately the general taxpayer will pay a large part of the bill.

As a method of increasing Government revenues, it is a tax on the lowest incomes in the country—provided they do not secure an increase in wages to compensate. In such case, however, it falls on the consumer, of which these beneficiaries are the largest group.

The answer to all these dilemmas is to abandon further building of the reserve fund and to put the whole business on a collect-and-pay-as-you-go basis. If my proposal were adopted, even the present payroll tax burden could be reduced during the next critical years.

c) Aside from the faults inherent in the "Federal Insurance System," the ultimate result of this new legislation will be to absorb or extinguish much of the "Independent Systems." The "Independent Systems" should be maintained and encouraged. They represent a flowering of American freedom and of moral growth. They have more efficient administration and usually provide greater benefits to their members than do either the "Federal Insurance System" or "State Systems." In the few instances where, by a change of jobs, a small number of beneficiaries under the "Independent Systems" might lose all or part of their rights under these systems, they can be picked up by the "State Systems."

d) Another point worth noting is that the powers vested in the Federal Administrator under these two bills could go a long way to extinguish the independence of the States in welfare activities. This can also result in an enormous increase in the number of State, Federal and other public officials necessary for administration. There are probably 30,000 State and Federal officials already engaged in administration even now.

A COURSE OF ACTION

5. My own opinion, having regard for our obligations to prevent suffering by the aged and their dependents due to the increased cost of living, together with the difficult economic situation we face from the cold war, is that we should go slowly and proceed as follows:

a) The further expansion of reserve funds should be abandoned, and the system should be placed on a pay-as-you-go basis.

b) Increase the benefits of the "Federal Insurance System" but, for the present, undertake none of the other expansions proposed in H.R. 2893 and thus greatly reduce the expenditures required.

c) Develop the "State Systems" based on need by further Federal grants to provide more adequately for the aged and dependents actually in need (the average now being only $42.02 per person per month, with some States as low as about $20.00 per month), and to enact none of the expansions in H.R. 2892.

The real and urgent problem is the need group. It is not solved now, nor can it be solved for many years, by the "Federal Insurance System"—even if that system can be made to work efficiently.

Whatever increased cost may be thus required in taking care of our needy and aged, it could be covered many times over by adopting the recommendations for better organization of the executive branch proposed by the Commission.

SEARCH FOR A SIMPLER SYSTEM

6. The Committee, in my opinion, should undertake to establish an independent research body to provide analyses of other possible systems. It should be given a year for study.

The reasons are:

a) On the organizational side, both the "State Systems" and the "Federal Insurance System" maintain expensive administrations of the same general problem. The administrative cost of the "Federal Insurance System" is likely, under this bill, to rise eventually to over $100,000,000 per annum. The "Independent Systems" do not overlap so extensively in the administration field, and usually are managed more economically.

b) In the financial support of these three systems, the overlap is very great. Many of the "Independent Systems," and the "Federal Insurance System," are based upon payroll contributions, and thus many contributors are in both systems, are being twice insured and will receive benefits from both systems. The people do not need to be provided for twice over, and where they are in both systems, their deduction burdens are very great and a menace to their families' standard of living.

c) It is obvious that the "State Systems" must be maintained for many years to come. It would be many, many years before complete and adequate coverage and benefits could be attained by the "Federal Insurance System." Its benefits, even under the new bill, are inadequate in many instances, and must, in any event, be supplemented by the "State Systems" based upon need.

d) A careful inquiry might disclose an entirely different system which would avoid the huge costs of administration and the duplication, which would substitute some other form of taxation, more simple and more direct for its support, and which would give more positive security to the aged than this complicated system.

It is worth looking into.

I attach hereto the pages of the Report of the Commission on Organization of the Executive Branch of the Government, and those of our Task Force (The Brookings Institution), which relate to some parts of this subject.

On Federal Grants-in-Aid

Letter to the Honorable Samuel K. McConnell, Jr.,
Committee on Education and Labor, House
of Representatives, Washington, D.C.
[June 22, 1949]

New York, New York
June 22, 1949

The Honorable Samuel K. McConnell, Jr.
Committee on Education and Labor
House of Representatives
Washington, D.C.

My dear Mr. Congressman:

I have your request that I should give you my views on Senate Bill 246, which is before your Committee. This bill provides for Federal "grants-in-aid" for primary and secondary education to the states under certain restrictions. It calls for an initial annual Federal expenditure of about $300,000,000 in addition to more than $2,000,000,000 annually, which is already being spent directly by the Federal Treasury for other educational purposes, for veterans, special schools, research work, scholarships, etc.

At the outset let me say that I doubt if anyone in the country is more devoted to the upbuilding of the educational system than myself. Also, I realize the economic limitations which produce backwardness of education in certain sections and the necessity of remedies in the broad national interest. The whole problem

41

is how to remedy the situation without great injury to the entire social and political fabric of the nation, including education.

One question immediately arises which came vividly to my attention in the recent investigation of the organization of the Executive Branch of the Government. The views which I express are, however, my own.

THE SYSTEM OF "GRANTS-IN-AID"

Before we consider this special bill, I believe we should first face certain broad questions involved in the whole method of the Federal Government's "grants-in-aid" to the states. The amount of these "grants-in-aid" has risen from $100,000,000 to $1,200,000,000 in twenty years. This does not include the billions being expended by the Federal Government by other methods for social and economic objectives. These "grants-in-aid" are, no doubt, all intended to do good, but the method of "grants-in-aid" contains grave dangers.

First. In all cases of "grants-in-aid," some are given to economically strong and self-sufficient states, well able to take care of themselves, as well as to those states which are economically unable to provide such necessary services and are thus backward in their educational work. The most appealing argument for such grants is based on situations in a small minority of backward states, yet by a sort of pork-barrel arrangement, the strong states are always also participating in "grants-in-aid."

Second. Any such "grants-in-aid" require the erection or expansion of Federal bureaucracy. But beyond this, they also require the erection or expansion of state bureaucracies. One of the consequences of all "grants-in-aid" is the organization of pressure groups, with branches in every state, constantly trying to expand and to get more "grants-in-aid" from the Federal Treasury.

Third. The economically strong or self-sufficient states, which are in a large majority, pay for their own "grants-in-aid" (and more) by Federal taxes, and whatever they receive back comes only after the cost of Federal bureaucratic middlemen is deducted.

Fourth. The "grants-in-aid" to economically self-sufficient states add just that much to the cost of the Federal Government, and the practice of requiring some sort of definite expenditure by the states often results in internal pressures to wasteful state expenditures.

Fifth. The inevitable effect of "grants-in-aid" is to place a Federal bureaucracy into dictatorship over the state or local administrations of these services. No matter what provision is made in the law to prevent such practices, it becomes inevitable that every such grant puts the camel's head of Federal control either under the tent of local self-government, or close to it. With all this we are steadily undermining the sense of responsibility and the fundamental basis of local self-government.

Finally, we may as well face the fact that the "grants-in-aid" system has become a prime instrument in centralizing the government of the people in Washington.

So much for observations on "grants-in-aid" in general.

If we are to attempt to cure education ills by the Federal "grants-in-aid" method, then the problem is how to do it with the least evil consequences. Therefore, after a review of the weaknesses in this bill in the above lights, I will make some suggestions for their remedy.

1. This particular bill (S. 246), in Section 2, makes drastic provisions against Federal bureaucratic dictations in the conduct of state educational facilities; but in Sections 7 and 8, it makes requirements of the states and their facilities which would almost immediately bring about the beginnings of Federal bureaucratic control. Even were this latter possibility not expected, we may be sure from past experience that complaints of state waste, inefficiency, or pressure groups will, sooner or later, result in drastic Federal controls. Moreover, the impelling forces within any Federal bureau will, sooner or later, break down any such limitations.

2. This bill, by a complicated economic formula involving

also the expenditures on education, endeavors to direct the major aid to backward states, which presumably have not the economic strength to care for their children.

3. But it also has the pork-barrel appendage of $5 for every child in the economically strong states as well. It thus tends to spread bureaucratic controls over the school system of the whole nation.

4. Aside from dependencies, there are apparently 19 states indicated in the backward category under this bill, although seven of those on that list should be able to care for their own children. The 36 remaining with the District of Columbia include roughly 80 percent of the children in the nation.

5. Based on the economic formula, the extra "grants-in-aid" are not based upon the essentials of proper educational standards, but certainly, in some cases, upon whether the citizens of the state desire to spend its revenues on education or on something else.

SUGGESTIONS

In order not to deny to children of the real backward states the opportunity they need, and also at the same time to avoid as many as possible of the evils of "grants-in-aid" and to produce economy which the nation badly needs, I suggest the following for consideration in this legislation:

a) There should be no general "grants-in-aid" to all states. All "grants-in-aid" should be limited in each case to the real backward states.

b) While the bill gives special attention to the backward states, to make the discrimination between them and the strong states, it is based upon involved economic calculations instead of upon certain specific standards of education which should be established.

Such specific standards could be based upon the average educational performance of, say, 30 of the most forward states. These standards should include teachers' fitness and salaries, the hours of attendance, and facilities. An additional standard should be that of nondiscrimination with reference to race or religion. And these standards, applied to the backward states, will need include another requirement. Some of the so-called educationally backward states are spending large sums on improvements such as highways, etc., which should be subordinated to the education of their children. These standards should not be difficult to determine through an appropriate independent commission. I use the term "average" as above, as a base, because it represents at any one time the real progress of the nation in this field.

The effect of such recommendations would be fivefold:

1. It would reduce the proposed appropriation of $300,000,-000 by some $150,000,000 by eliminating the nonbackward states.

2. It would limit both Federal and state costs of government through unnecessary bureaucratic expansion.

3. By eliminating the nonbackward states, it would keep the camel's head out of probably 80 percent of the nation's educational tents, and it would confine its entry into the states with insufficient economic resources.

4. By the focusing of public opinion, it would stimulate some of the backward states who have resources to meet the national standards.

5. By limiting its operation to the backward states, it would curb nation-wide drives upon the Congress for new and increasing "grants-in-aid" by special groups and interests, which are inevitable from any general "grants-in-aid" method of government operation.

And let me add that of all the accomplishments of our Republic, the greatest has been our educational system in the strong states. It ranks above that of all other nations. It is the product of private effort, of local and state government. To place a Federal bureaucracy over the whole national system will be, in my mind, a disaster to educational progress—no matter what legal limits are put on it or what advantages are painted.

I agree wholeheartedly with some of General Eisenhower's recent observations in which he pointed out that this act will become another vehicle for the believers in paternalism, additional national centralization of power, and that the very attempts at safeguards are admission of the dangers inherent in it.

What we need in the national interest is to bring the backward states up to the national level of educational care for children and preserve the nation from the evils inherent in the "grants-in-aid" system.

I am, with deep respect,

Yours truly,

HERBERT HOOVER

On Views as to Old-Age Assistance

Letter to Senator H. Alexander Smith,
Princeton, New Jersey
[December 15, 1949]

New York, New York
December 15, 1949

The Honorable H. Alexander Smith
81 Princeton Street
Princton, New Jersey

My dear Alex:

My present views as to Old-Age Assistance revolve around several parts:

1. The country wants and needs old-age protection to those over 65 years of age.

2. The late labor settlements line the employers behind the Government contributory system.

3. It needs to be extended in coverage and benefits.

4. It must remain a contributory system, or it will get entirely out of hand.

5. It should be put on a "pay-as-you-go" basis.

a) Congress should each year estimate for a year ahead the amount of wage tax necessary to support it and impose that amount;

b) It should appropriate the necessary funds each year;

c) Congress should use the present reserve fund as a balance

47

wheel to make up for deficiencies or to receive surpluses, but not build it up further.

6. There is no such thing as an actuarial calculation or reserve fund basis for this service. The Government cannot insure itself.

7. The use of so-called reserve funds in part for current expenses of the Government by placing bonds in trust unquestionably imposes a twice payment by the beneficiaries because the general taxpayer (which means in large part the beneficiaries) must redeem the Government bonds in the present system.

8. Under the present system the Congress has little control of the rightfulness, honesty or policies. That must be regained through the appropriation process.

9. I have an idea that the whole distribution of insurance benefits should be made through the state "old-age assistance systems."

a) This will save much duplication in administration costs as the states must continue their own "old-age assistance systems" in any event.

b) This would allow them to make proper *supplements* from "old-age assistance" to the insurance benefits so as to provide adequate amounts for living.

c) The states could then well make adjustments in the amounts of *their supplements* so as not to pay persons having adequate old-age protection from other quarters, such as industrial additions to "insurance" benefits; direct pension services of Federal, state, municipal, universities, hospitals, and so forth; and income taxpayers over certain limits.

d) All this would place the contact of the individual in control of state governments and, by removing the Federal Government from that contact, would stop a lot of Federal mischief.

e) By this method of imposing determination of *supplementary aid* from the states on the states as *additions* (if necessary) *to insurance benefits*, the whole system would probably be within Federal and state resources.

f) The states could adjust their supplements to the conditions of living within the state. For instance, the cost of living is much less in the Southern states than in the Northern states.

It is my feeling that, in time, the contributory (so-called insurance) system would be carrying the bulk of the load. In any event, the states would under this plan (like the employers) be advocates of building up the contributory system.

Yours faithfully,

HERBERT HOOVER

On Representative Government*

American Druggist

[*July 1950*]

SUCCESSFUL representative government depends on the existence of two major political parties:—one to carry the responsibility of government administration; the other to provide the fundamental checks and balances by opposing and ventilating the administrative actions. The two-party system also provides an anvil of debate in legislative halls where the merits and demerits of proposals can be hammered out.

Benjamin Franklin once remarked: "By the collision of different sentiments, sparks of truth fly out and political light is obtained."

When a debate is over and some conclusion reached by a majority on a public question, either in the legislative halls or at the ballot box, the Constitution still stands there with all its checks and balances to protect the minority. We have no arbitrary government by the majority. And over all government and politics, there is a balance of power greater than all this machinery of procedures, whether elections, debates or laws. That is, just plain morals.

Our two-party system reorients itself as new major issues emerge. At one time they were oriented on the most fundamental of all freedoms—slavery. For many years they both fairly well represented 19th century Liberalism with the tariff question about the only difference. Then came the train of Col-

* Reprinted from *American Druggist* by permission of the publishers.

lectivism over the world. Today the people, and consequently the political parties, are being reoriented to meet the major question of State operation or dictation to economic life—in popular expression, to the "right" or to the "left."

Again it comes up to the citizen himself to examine this issue, to support the side his conclusions bring him. My personal opinion is that if the citizen loves freedom and wants to perpetuate the American System of life, he will vote on the "right."

So a citizen has a complex duty. He ought to learn to express opinions and to make up his own mind pro and con on the principal public issues. He ought never to miss the ballot box. And when he casts his vote for somebody, he should weigh that somebody in the scales of morals—which includes intellectual integrity.

On Urging and Stimulating Voting

Statement Recorded for Mutual Broadcasting System,
New York City
[October 11, 1948]

THE weakest link in the whole chain of protections to liberty is the vote. Other protections can be provided by law and officials designated to look after them.

The first step in protection of representative government is the vote. But that act is voluntary. If people do not go to the polls, freedom will die at its roots.

It is always a mystery to me why at every election there must be urging by a thousand voices: "Go to the Polls." Either our people must be absent-minded or not concerned with their own safety. You may be sure that every fellow with an "ism" or a wild "do-not-like" will be there. If you want to neutralize him, then go and vote.

On Advertising

Remarks before the Advertising Clubs of New York City
[November 14, 1949]

YOURS is a vital part in economic freedom. This being a friendly meeting, I will not discuss whether or not we still have it. I will at least assume it will come again.

Advertising was not always looked upon as a vital part of a free economic system. There was a time when you had about the same economic and moral position as the barker outside the circus tent. But the economists came along with the idea that one of the motive forces in economic progress was "wish," "choice," "want," and "desire." Very quickly you took over the job of stimulating "desire" and "choice." You also engage in creating good will in order to make "desire" and "choice" stand hitched. From all these torments of "desire" and "choice" demand was created, and from demand increased production arose and thence around the cycle we landed with increased standards of living.

Indeed, our standards of living are built up like cake. The lower layers are bare food, clothing, and shelter. After the Garden of Eden episode, sheer necessity served to stir up enough emotions at these lower levels to keep that part of "desire" moving. It is to create the top layers of the cake that you have come in. By stirring up "desire" and "choice" for ten thousand things, you put on more and more layers of the cake. The automobile is one of the top layers. If advertising had not lifted that "desire" to a mass production industry, few people would have gotten its joys, its excitements and dangers to life. If you had been present at the first revolutionary discovery in transporta-

53

tion—the wheeled cart—you gentlemen would have speeded up the advance of civilization a few centuries. Also I suggest on the credit side that you have advanced or at least spread the arts. Without your subsidies to publications and the radio, the writers and the artists would not have risen to the top layers of the cake. For you have emancipated the artists and the writers from the slavery of being compelled to seek a hall bedroom from some noble patron, to eat at his second table, and to write flattering dedications to him. And now the writers and artists have risen to the high estate of taking part in your beguiling of "desire" and "choice." I do not mention the musicians as I get no impression of advancing civilization out of the singing commercial.

You have some sins to answer for. I will not introduce discord into this happy occasion by mentioning all of them. Sometime, I have a dreamy hope you will cease using the scenery to urge pills on me when I am seeking those solitudes where fish alone can dwell. But I do thank you for not placing electric signs over those spots.

On Receiving an Award by New York Board of Trade

Remarks before the New York Board of Trade Dinner, the Waldorf Astoria, New York City
[October 18, 1949]

I HAVE had some doubt about what a recipient of an award ought to say. I suspicion that inside this award there is an intellectual gadget that presses the recipient to say something that would justify his having received it.

Ruminating over this problem of what to say, it seemed to me that the real test of whether the recipient has said something justifying the award is whether his remarks make a page one, column one, double headline in the morning papers.

So I have been haunted for days with a subconscious search for subject or eloquent phrase which would land at that spot.

In that search I examined the current press for what sort of remarks from speakers got page one, double column. I found they all relate to ideas of alarm, emergency, crisis, warning, purge, execution, condemnation, or the current practice of diplomats in denouncing other governments. So I looked over those intellectual provinces to see if I could find a shot that might land.

For instance, I thought it ought to shock the world if I said something about the balancing of the Federal budget. That, however, does not seem to have clicked in the headlines for the last eighteen years.

I also considered a mordant economic discourse on why loans by our taxpayers to foreign governments physically cannot and never will be repaid. Then it occurred to me that Santa Claus is a person of far more favorable reputation than Shylock, certainly in the international field. It also occurred to me we could choose either reputation at exactly the same price. That idea, however, has not been news since the first World War.

I thought perhaps I might define the welfare state. But I feel it would be respectful to concede the President has a monopoly of shocks from that quarter.

It would be natural for me to talk about the reorganization of the Federal Government. Indeed, it is about the only issue in which there is complete unity of all political parties, races, religions, and government bureaus. Its merit has the same acceptance of universal merit which our grandmothers established for mustard plasters. But it has the same sort of exception—the fellow to be reorganized. The wails and miseries of its application today take all the headlines, not the reasons for reorganization.

I thought also I might appeal for more unity in world affairs —by way of discussing the United Nations or Union Now or World Federation. But there is no derivative of the Latin root of unity which would make a headline any more. It is vitriolic international conversation that gets page 1, column 1.

I might speak of the Point 4 program, whereby American private enterprise is presumed to go abroad and fill the world with milk and honey. I surmised, however, you already know that by double taxation at home. Business now has more than it can bear without seeking to expose itself twice more to the tax mercies of two countries at the same time. To suggest a mitigation of taxes between these two stools might help but you cannot make headline stuff of double taxation in this world, to say nothing of such quadruple taxation.

For all these reasons and for the good of your digestion, I will speak on none of these subjects.

I will content myself with expressing my deep gratitude for the honor which you have conferred upon me.

PART II

FOREIGN POLICIES

The Voice of World Experience

*Address before the American Newspaper Publishers
Association, the Waldorf Astoria,
New York City
[April 27, 1950]*

I T IS a great honor to address the Editors and Publishers of the United States. You are the most powerful of all influences in our country.

My subject on this occasion arises from my suspicion that the world in its tumults has abandoned most of its acceptance of history as a guidepost.

There are plenty of voices about but the voice of world experience seems to have become stilled.

I have had to do with the boiling economic, social, and political forces during two world wars and their aftermaths. I propose for a few moments to add some of the voices of world experience to the present clamor. I shall explore four samples, one each from the economic, social, political, and international field.

SOME ECONOMIC EXPERIENCE

In the economic field there are as you well know many shrill voices proclaiming that our American economic system is outmoded. They say it was born of undesirable parents, such as American Individualism and a French lady named *Laissez-Faire*. They accuse the ghost of Adam Smith as having had something to do with the matter. They conclude our system is of the jungle or dog-eat-dog variety.

It might be observed that the alternative offered us is a drink mixed by three different ghosts. That is, the shade of Karl Marx with his socialism; the shade of Mussolini with his dictated and planned economy; the spook of Lord John Maynard Keynes with his "operation Cuttlefish." That comprises "managed currency," peacetime inflation by "deficit spending" and perpetual endowment for bureaucrats. And we have contributed an American ideology. That is give-away programs. It might be called the New Generosity. It is not yet a ghost. However, the handiwork of the ghosts and their auxiliaries furnish you most of your Page One.

I am not going to repeat the old and valid defenses of the American Economic System; I may mention that in recent years we have taken strong drinks from the three "hants" I have mentioned, and from the New Generosity, all mixed with varying amounts of pure water from the American System.

THE ECONOMIC REVOLUTION

Be all that as it may, my purpose at this moment is to call your attention to a less obvious world experience.

Sixty years ago our American System was divorced from the *Laissez-Faire* lady. We started proceedings in 1887 when we created the Interstate Commerce Commission, thereby initiating the control of natural monopolies. But far more revolutionary was the Anti-Trust Act of 1890.

Western Europe has never had effective Anti-Trust laws. To the contrary, there grew up in those countries a maze of state-favored private trade restraints, combinations, trusts and cartels. That form of economic organization sought profits by fixing prices and by control of production and distribution.

Under our revolutionized American System, competition fairly well remained the restless pillow of progress. It had to seek profits from improved technology and lowered costs of production.

In time, Western Europe, without the full pressure of competition, lost much of the impulse to improve methods and equipment. Plants became obsolete; standards of living stagnated.

In contrast, our technology with one hundred times as many inventing laboratories and a thousand times more trained technicians has steadily improved its tools. Our standards of living increased with cheaper costs and more goods. Our system was dynamic; theirs was static.

Finally, Western Europe, with its obsolete plants, its inability to compete in world trade, except at the expense of labor, was desperate. It took to hard drinking of the potions from the shades of Marx, Mussolini and Keynes—plus the New Generosity.

Our American System continues to produce despite periodic indulgence in these drinks. It does it despite two world wars, innumerable interferences with incentives, and a government take of 60 or 70 percent of its savings. It still retains the dynamic power to provide the greatest and widest spread of comfort to our people that the world has ever known. That is, if we would join Alcoholics Anonymous and quit mixed drinks.

Lest any dangerous thought flash through your minds, I am recalling this experience exclusively to you as publishers and editors.

AN EXPERIENCE IN SOCIOLOGY

Now lest someone think all this is economics without humanism, I offer an experience on the social side. It is punctuated today by the siren voices calling for "security from the cradle to the grave."

Security from the cradle to about 18 or 20 years of age, and from about 65 to the grave, has always been sacred to the American people.

The training of our children, the care of our aged and the unfortunate have been a part of our system since the founding of the Republic. It is part of our civilization. The governmental part, however, needs some repairs.

But the voice of experience which I wish to recall relates to the idea of security for the middle group—say, from 20 to 65 years of age. We have less than 70,000,000 providers in this group, and they must provide for 80,000,000 children, aged, sick, nonproductive Government employees and their wives. It is solely from the energies of this middle group, their inventions and their productivity that can come the support of the young, the old and the sick—and the Government employees.

Unless there is the constant pressure of competition on this group between 20 and 65 plus the beckoning of fairies and rewards, to stimulate incentives and work, the children and the aged will be the victims. This middle group can find its own security only in a free but tough system of risk and self-reliance. It can be destroyed by taxes and the four mixed drinks.

Experience calls sorrowful confirmation of all this. My recollection is that the Lord remarked to Adam something about sweat.

Be that as it may, there is convincing evidence from the British experience of trying to include the middle group in blessed security. Their incentives to sweat have diminished under that illusion. The needed leadership of the middle group in production and distribution is being slowly destroyed. Otherwise they would not need lean on the New Generosity.

There are also some lessons of experience to be had from Russia where the grave is close to the cradle. There, in order to get production, 15,000,000 people are compelled to work in slave camps under the whip.

AN EXPERIENCE IN THE POLITICAL FIELD

The voice of world experience also calls loudly as to organization of the political field. In 1938, I spent some months on the Continent inquiring "how come" the failure of fifteen new democracies created after the First World War.

The downfall of these representative governments was due in part to the drinks compounded by the three ghosts. But there was another step in their arrival at chaos, which contains a potent experience for the United States.

There had grown up in their legislatures a multitude of splinter parties. There were all the way from five to fifteen of them. In consequence, there was no responsible majority. Governments were driven to improvised legislative coalitions, which could only agree upon negative policies and give-away programs. In each coalition small foreign-controlled tricky groups played a part. In confusion and despair, their peoples welcomed the Man on Horseback.

Even though old-time religion, it is worth repeating that the preservation of representative government requires two major political parties.

I am not going to deliver a history of the rifts between major parties in the United States. So you may relax. I might mention that once upon a time, say for a period of about 60 years, the members of both of our major political parties were, in large majority, liberals in the 19th century sense. They quarreled mostly over the tariff but not over ideologies.

However, since Lenin's implication that the hermit crab, by seizing the shell of another animal, knew his business, the term "liberal" has lost its soul. Its cheerful spirit of less power in government and more freedom of men has passed to the world beyond.

Nor am I going to try your after-dinner souls with ideological definitions—not even the "Welfare State." The real ideological definition has already been made instinctively by the common tongue of all nations where free speech still has a part in their proceedings. That effective but perhaps unrefined definition is "right wing" and "left wing."

The point I am concerned with here is that from the ideological tumults stirred by the three shades and their helpers, our major American political parties have been in large degree reoriented into these new compartments of "right" and "left."

I do not charge the real Communists to the American left wing. They are agents of a foreign government.

If a Man from the Moon, who knew the essentials of representative government, came as a total stranger to the United States, he would say some obvious things within the first week or two.

He would say to the Republican Party: There is no room for

you on the left. You must be the party of the right, or you will split into ineffective fragments.

And with equal emphasis he would say to the Democrats: Your die is cast. You are the party of the left, or you will likewise split into futile factions.

He would say to some members of both Parties: You are not in your proper spiritual homes.

He would say that in all this ideological tumult, if there cannot be a reasonably cohesive body of opinion in each major party, you are on a blind road where there is no authority in the ballot box or in government.

He would say that if you want confirmation look at fifteen European countries where representative government was torn to shreds.

AN EXPERIENCE IN THE INTERNATIONAL FIELD

I need not remind you that our page one international issue is Communist Russia. There are seven phases of this experience which I must recall before I come to a proposal of action.

The first phase of experience with Russia began under the Czars. Since Peter the Great they steadily have expanded their reach of Empire over the largest land mass in the world. Their method was that of a burglar going down a hall. If there was no one in the first room, he took everything including the doorknob. If he found someone in the second room who protested, he weighed the strength of the protester and might leave part of the furniture. If he found an armed man in the third room, he closed the door and waited.

Lenin and Stalin added a new apparatus for the robber. They now make the man in the second room a Party member and rob him later and by degrees. They now put the armed man in the third room asleep with a non-aggression pact or a promise of peace. Thus, he neglects his weapons. In any event they steal his secrets.

The second phase of this experience with Russia was a period of sixteen years during which four Presidents and seven Secretaries of State opposed our having any relations with this malignant government. Their attitude was that when our neighbors are living a life of spiritual and other disrepute, we do not attack them. But we can hold up standards in the world a little better if we do not invite them into our homes by so-called diplomatic recognition.

The third historical phase arrived when our left wingers had their way in our relations with Communist Russia. They produced the recognition of the Soviet in 1933. They produced the alliance with Russia in 1941. They produced the appeasement of Russia in Western Europe until its reversal by President Truman and Secretary Byrnes in 1945. I will not join in the explanations about China. Up to now there is agreement on only one point. We lost the game—400 million to nothing.

Many of our left wingers were not consciously doing all this. They were just trigger-happy to anything new in the ideological line.

Lest anyone think I am a recent convert in these views, I may cite that just nine years and 63 days ago in a public address I warned the American people that collaboration with Stalin to bring freedom to mankind was a gargantuan jest. I used the wrong adjective. I should have said tragic. For as a result, instead of the expansion of liberty, we witness a dozen nations and 600 million human beings enslaved.

The fourth phase of this experience was that Soviet Russia has since our recognition violated more than 35 solemnly signed agreements.

The fifth phase of this experience has been with the Communists in the United Nations. That Charter for which we hoped so much contains lengthy pledges to the independence of nations, to human liberty and to non-aggression. About a dozen provisions of that Charter have been violated either in spirit or in letter by Soviet Russia. The Kremlin has reduced the United Nations to a propaganda forum for the smearing of free peoples. It has been defeated in its major purpose as a maker of peace and good will.

The sixth phase of this experience is that we now find ourselves in an expensive and dangerous cold war. We conduct the battle with subsidies to beguile peoples to rectitude from internal Communism. A year ago we made the Atlantic Military Pact. The expressed hope was that although there was no commitment to go to war, these nations would build up their own arms to adequately defend their own rooms. In persistence to an old habit, we are taking up the check.

In the meantime we learn that our first defense—the atomic bomb—has been stolen from us.

The final phase of our experience with Russia is the belated realization that this is not one world. It is two worlds. The one world idea seems to be lost in the secret files.

One world is militaristic, imperialistic, atheistic, and without compassion. The other world still holds to belief in God, free nations, human dignity, and peace.

SOME PROPOSITIONS

Now to come to the point of all this. The American people ought to take a cold and objective look at this experience before we go any further.

This look should be directed to the fact that more and more the burdens of defending free men and nations are being thrust upon the American people, who are only one-sixth the population of the globe. We are becoming more and more isolated as the sole contender in this cold war. We are steadily losing ground because the non-Communist states are being picked off one by one or they are compromising with the Communists. Our countrymen are in a fog as to what, where and when all this leads to.

What the world needs today is a definite, spiritual mobilization of the nations who believe in God against this tide of Red agnosticism. It needs a moral mobilization against the hideous ideas of the police state and human slavery. The world needs mobilization against this creeping Red imperialism. The United States needs to know who are with us in the cold war against these practices, and whom we can depend on.

Therefore, I have a proposal to make.

I suggest that the United Nations should be reorganized without the Communist Nations in it. If that is impractical then a definite New United Front should be organized of those peoples who disavow Communism, who stand for morals and religion, and who love freedom.

This is specifically not a proposed extension of a military alliance or any color of it. It is a proposal based solely upon moral, spiritual and defense foundations. It is a proposal to redeem the concept of the United Nations to the high purpose for which it was created. It is a proposal for moral and spiritual co-operation of God-fearing free nations.

If the free nations join together, they have many potent moral, spiritual and even economic weapons at their disposal. They would unlikely ever need such weapons. Such a phalanx of free nations could come far nearer to making a workable relation with the other half of the two worlds than the United States can ever do alone.

By collective action we could much more effectively keep their conspiring agents and bribers out of all our borders and out of our laboratories.

It may be the non-Communist world is not willing to take such a vital stand. At least it would clarify what we have to do.

The test I propose is the logical and practical end of total diplomacy. It would make diplomacy dynamic and lessen the dangers of the American people. All this may give pain to some people. But by their cries ye shall know them.

IN CONCLUSION

My friends, I am not disheartened by all this recall of disturbing experience. We must retain our faith in Western civilization. In support of that faith we are perhaps a slow but a resolute and intelligent people. We have the greatest organ of education known to man—a free press. You can dissolve much of our confusions and frustrations.

And in rejecting an atheistic other world, I am confident that the Almighty God will be with us.

The United Nations and World Peace

Dedication of the William Allen White Memorial,
Emporia, Kansas
[July 11, 1950]

SINCE your invitation to address you on this occasion in honor of William Allen White, a momentous and sad trial has come to our country. An attack has been made on the peace of the world. I have no doubt that every loyal American will support the President.

Tonight I wish to speak upon some of the problems of lasting peace, together with Mr. White's relations to them.

PART I

THE CHARACTER AND SERVICE OF MR. WHITE

But first let me say something of the life and character of Mr. White. All of his adult life he was the editor of a newspaper in this town. At the same time he was a powerful leader of American thought and of things of the spirit.

To refresh my memory, I have gone through the files of hundreds of communications between us over a third of a century. They revive again our comradeship in many common causes. They bring to life again the sparkle of his expression and his wit; the breadth of his outlook on our country; his keen insight

68

into the forces moving in the world; and the depth of his devotion to America and to all mankind. They reflect his unflagging devotion to his friends which was so much a part of his character and spirit. They prove his rare ability to appraise forces and clarify confusions. And every page raises again the sense of personal loss at his passing and the loss to his country of his superlative mind and character.

William Allen White was an unvarnished nineteenth-century Liberal—something far different from those who would travel under that cloak today. His was a never-ceasing gospel of personal liberty. He was opposed to every Governmental encroachment upon it. He opposed every domination of free men, whether by business, labor, farmers, or by group action anywhere, or at any time. For half a century his was the great voice of the Midwest which still clung to building progress through freedom of men's minds and spirits.

But above all, these files constantly reflect his efforts for peace for our country and for the world.

THE PARIS PEACE CONFERENCE

We were together at the heartbreaking peacemaking at Versailles. We grieved over its political settlements. At that time also, we, each in his own field, had to deal with the bloody rise of Communism in the world. Its horrible philosophy and its portents to mankind were large in our minds even then.

THE LEAGUE OF NATIONS

After Versailles, I joined with Mr. White in urging American entry into the League of Nations. He remained constant to that purpose long after America had relegated it to the Never-Never Land. He stuck to the ideal of international organization to preserve peace as a great moral and spiritual necessity if civilization were not to be destroyed. He hoped the League could be freed of its chains and in the end serve its great purpose.

OPPOSITION TO AMERICA JOINING IN THE SECOND WORLD WAR

Again, when the Second World War cast its dread shadow over the earth, he and I, until Pearl Harbor, were opposed to America's joining in that war. When war came we both gave undeviating support to our Government. Mr. White was no isolationist. He was not only devoted to world organization to preserve peace, but he did much to secure aid in materials for Britain so that Hitler should not triumph.

We were stiffly challenged in that great prewar debate. But he never lost confidence that the judgment of future generations would be in our favor.

That debate had many facets, one of which has a direct bearing on today's problems. That occasion arose with the proposed strange alliance between the United States and Communist Russia at the time of Hitler's attack on Stalin in June, 1941. Mr. White and I both protested against that alliance. We stated that the British were then relieved of danger of defeat because of the diversion of Hitler's armies. We said the result of our joining with Russia would be to expand Communism and diminish liberty in the world. The record is clear that we both foresaw the only hope of peace to the free world was the mutual exhaustion of these two dreadful despotisms.

We agreed that when the day came that they were sufficiently exhausted to listen to the military, economic and moral powers of the United States—at that moment, and at that moment only, could the United States promote a just and lasting peace.

Many other Americans held similar views. President Truman, then a Senator, on June 23, 1941, expressed somewhat these ideas.

Confirmation of the rightness of that position has already been the verdict of many masters of history. Seldom has advice in war been so quickly justified by the development of world events. With that wrong turning, the United States was to prove powerless to bring lasting peace.

PART II

THE PRESENT CRISIS

The questions arise in every American's mind: Can lasting peace come to this world? Are we forever to be diverted, from the high purposes of civilization, to support huge armies and sacrifice our sons?

I pray hourly that we may not again be involved in another general war. There is some comfort in the fact that a general war must have an attainable end that can be strategically possible. There is no general military victory strategically possible for the Kremlin.

But the men in the Kremlin are not always sane men. At the moment, they are making a try-on to test the limits of appeasement and to test the solidarity of the non-Communist members of the United Nations. We must meet that test.

PART III

SOME APPRAISALS

It is vital to our future that, without petty criticism, we appraise objectively these forces and some lessons from the past.

Today, as I advance toward the end of my life span, after 35 years given to the problems of peace and war, I should fail in my duty did I not speak out on these questions.

THE INTERNATIONAL PURPOSES OF COMMUNISM

Today there is but one enemy of peace in the world. We should coldly examine this great malignant force.

It is only about thirty years since Lenin, its leader, repeatedly and publicly confirmed its philosophy, its ideas and methods, in international relations. On one occasion, Lenin said: "As long as capitalism remains we cannot live in peace. In the end one or the other will triumph—a funeral requiem will be sung over the Soviet Republic or over world capitalism. . . ." Again he said: "We have to use any ruse, dodges, tricks, cunning, unlawful method, concealment, and veiling of the truth." And again: "The basic rule is to exploit conflicting interests . . . to dodge and maneuver." And again: "Religion is the opiate of the people."

That does not sound like the Sermon on the Mount.

Lest anyone think Stalin and his Politburo are reformed men, I may remind you of the repeated oaths at Lenin's tomb to carry out every word of that gospel. And, indeed, you may find the expansion of these evil ideas in their writings and their resolutions down to this day.

Those who dismiss these statements as merely the heat of revolution or in blind hope they have been abandoned should review step-by-step the actions of these men over the last 11 years. The men of the Kremlin have in so short a time violated over 35 solemnly signed treaties. They have subjected a dozen nations and 600,000,000 human beings in those nations to slavery. Their persecution of all religious leaders has never ceased to this day. Except to the blind, there stands out the cunning "dodges, tricks, unlawful methods, and veiling of the truth" by which the Allied leaders were fooled at Teheran, Yalta and Potsdam. And I could also remind you that today there are unending Fifth Columns in every nation. I could recite that at times they have even penetrated into the high ranks in our own Government. I could review the convictions of Hiss, Coplon, and Fuchs; Gold's confession; the Canadian spy case; the repeated jail sentences of American Communists for conspiracy against us. Today, Red Russia threatens the world with greater armies than all the rest of the world put together.

But what more confirmation do we need of Lenin's and Stalin's philosophy and method than the events of the past 15 days?

This is the force with which we now have to deal.

TWO WARS

We should also coldly re-examine our experience from having fought two gigantic wars at fearful cost in resources and in lives. The valor of our men won great battles. But we have won no lasting peace. However, from these sacrifices we can deduce some vital truths.

I suggest to you a fundamental truism. War is justified only as an instrument for a specific consequence. That consequence for America was lasting peace. In four directions we strayed from that major objective.

First. Both wars proved that we cannot change ideas in the minds of men and races with machine guns or battleships. Our purposes were confused in both wars by crusades with glorious phrases about the personal freedom of man. Ideas in nations are rooted in their racial history, their very mores. Ideological wars are no more capable of settling anything than the thousand years of crusades and religious wars of the Middle Ages. Such wars have no ending and no victory. The way of life of a people must come from within; it cannot be compelled from without.

Whatever the present events may bring, I suggest we never again enter upon such crusades. If the Communist states like their slave ideology, we should engage in no loss of American lives to free them from it. Communism is a force of evil. It contains within itself the germs which will in time destroy it.

We should say, "Our concern is only that you keep your armed men within your own borders. As to your Fifth Columns, our jails are our peace device."

Second. Our second departure from our major purpose was concentration on winning military battles. Winning battles which do not drive to the major purpose of lasting peace are battles lost.

In support of these views, may I quote today's greatest of American military writers, Mr. Hanson Baldwin of *The New York Times'* staff, who in a recent book says,

"The United States has fought wars differently from other peoples. We have fought for the immediate victory, not for the ultimate peace. . . . we have had no . . . well-defined political objective to chart our military action.

"We fought to win—period. We did not remember that wars are merely an extension of politics by other means. . . ."

The alliance with Stalin in 1941, to which I referred, is a profound example.

I will not elaborate but I recommend that you read Mr. Baldwin's little book.

If we should be forced—and I pray not—to engage in general war, our military strategy must be held to our single major purpose, which is lasting peace.

Third. In our political settlements after both wars, we departed from our true path and left many nations in such a plight as to become the prey of others. We yielded to the spirits of greedy imperialism in other nations and of vindictiveness and revenge.

We sowed the dragon's teeth of still another war.

Fourth. Truly, in both wars we realized that lasting peace could come only from suppression of aggression and from disarmament. The League of Nations and the United Nations were set up in that hope. The tragedy of the League was that it was turned into an instrument to protect imperial spoils of war. The tragedy of the United Nations was that it turned into an instrument to protect Red imperialism.

PART IV

THE MAKING OF LASTING PEACE

During 1942 and 1943, after America was in the Second World War, Mr. White, Hugh Gibson and I joined in urging that when the shooting stopped the world must try again to build a new and effective organization to preserve peace. Perhaps vainly, we believed we could distill from world experience some lessons on how it should be done.

From the experience of a hundred years, including the Congress of Vienna and Versailles, we said to obtain lasting peace that political peace with the enemy states must be made first; that a period of two or three years should elapse for emotions to cool and thought to ripen. We stated the principles for political settlements from which, when men's passions had abated, the Dragon's Teeth could not spring again. We asserted that the attitude of great nations, including Communist Russia, must become clear before an adequate world organization could be built.

THE UNITED NATIONS

But the United Nations was handicapped by being launched into a morass where there was no peace to preserve.

Still more tragic is that for five years the United Nations has with the Kremlin's gospel been made an instrument to provoke fear and hate among and within the nations of the earth. The purpose of Soviet Russia is not to carry out the four times repeated pledge in the United Nations Charter to establish the independence of nations and peace on earth.

Forty-two times Soviet Russia has used its veto to thwart important efforts toward peace. The Kremlin representatives have denied membership in the United Nations to 9 anti-Communist nations. Thirty-four times they have walked out of meetings in an effort to coerce the members into accepting Communist China into its very seat of power—the Security Council —which would further communize the organization and give another veto to Russia.

Yet if we survey the world, we find that although one-third of the people on earth have been subdued to Communism, there still remain 60 non-Communist nations, comprising two-thirds of the people on the earth, who yet cling to belief in God and the independence of nations.

PART V

THE WAY OUT

Today our hopes of lasting peace lie in a new direction of national policies. The first of these is to reorganize the United Nations.

Two months ago, in an address to the Newspaper Publishers, I stated that our problem was to mobilize the economic, moral and spiritual strength of these 60 non-Communist peoples for lasting peace. I suggested that the UN stop appeasement and Soviet domination. I proposed if that agency was to function in its task of lasting peace it must be reorganized without the Communists in it. I pointed out that the United States was steadily being saddled with the sole responsibility of defending the independence of nations. I stated that thus the United States would be part of a phalanx, and not become a single spear.

Two months ago it looked as though it might be a long time before the world would realize this inevitable necessity. At that time the officials of the UN and our State Department unanimously and loudly denounced my proposal. I will not, on this occasion, pursue that point.

Today, the mobilization of non-Communist nations free from Russian domination is slowly unfolding. The Security Council has called upon its members to join in repelling the aggression against Korea. Some 42 members have given that call their moral support. Three other nations have so far joined with us in the military measures of that task. We shall soon know how much the world is prepared to meet this issue.

The non-Communist world is now faced with three possible courses if it would have peace:

Shall it go to war to wipe Communism from the face of the earth? I have stated that my answer is "No."

Should we return to the illusion that the Kremlin has changed its gospel and will work for world peace through the United Nations? That would seem futile.

Shall we try to build the United Nations so as to confine Communism to the peoples already enslaved, estop military aggression and trust to time for this evil to abate? My answer is "YES."

Alternatively we must crawl into isolation and defend the Western Hemisphere alone. That would be less than a secure peace.

The answers to these questions, however, may not be in our hands.

While our purpose must be to isolate this malignant force, we might even say to the Kremlin:

"When you have proved that your purpose is peace and that you have abandoned the purpose of aggression and hate, we would be glad to have you stop your walk-out of the United Nations, but never again may you have power to thwart the march of peace."

CLARIFICATION OF NATIONAL POLICIES

But beyond all immediate action, if we are to take part in bringing lasting peace to the world, we and the United Nations must have clarification of thinking and determination of purpose. We cannot successfully cope with present world problems or secure a lasting peace without consistent and clearly defined policies and objectives which we are prepared to support and defend. Military strength is no substitute for sound policy.

I give you an example. Over a century ago our country announced the Monroe Doctrine. We never flinched from its support. The world knew what we meant and few have ever tried to breach it. It has contributed to peace throughout all these years.

I will not pursue the subject further at this time. You might get an idea of what I mean by reading the second, third, and fourth verses of the first chapter of the Book of Genesis.

In the meantime, may I recall to you a sentence of mine which had wide distribution in a former time of trial.

"Pray hard, work hard, sleep hard, and play hard. Do it courageously and cheerfully. We have a cause to win."

I believe that, were William Allen White among us today, he would not speak very differently—but he would have said all this with a grace and skill and gentleness for those were the gifts that the good Lord gave to him at birth and which he always used to the advantage of his country.

On Views on the China Situation

Letters to Senator William F. Knowland,
Washington, D.C.
[December 31, 1949]

New York, New York
December 31, 1949

Honorable William F. Knowland
United States Senate
Washington, D.C.

My dear Senator:

I have your request for my views on the China situation.

There is merit in the contention that the continuous pressures upon the anti-Communist National Government of China, beginning in 1943, to take the Communists into that government contributed to the breakdown of prestige and strength of Chiang Kai-shek, and the encouragement of Mao Tse-tung. Despite all this, your question still remains. What to do next?

It is my strong belief that we should not recognize the Communist Government of China; that we must continue to recognize and support the National Government; that we should, if necessary, give it naval protection to the possessions of Formosa, the Pescadores, and possibly Hainan islands.

Among many reasons are:

(1) A wall against Communism in the Pacific;

(2) The defense of Japan and the Philippines;

(3) The prevention of the Chinese Legations and Consulates in the United States (and such other countries as agree with us) becoming nests of Communist conspiracies;

(4) The prevention of another Communist permanent member of the United Nations Security Council, with its dangerous implications to that body;

(5) The dangers of Chinese Communist participation in formulating peace with Japan;

(6) By maintaining at least a symbol of resistance, we would have a better basis for salvation of Southeastern Asia;

(7) There would be at least a continued hope of some time turning China in the paths of freedom again.

Yours faithfully,

HERBERT HOOVER

New York, New York
December 31, 1949

My dear Senator:

I do not think there is any purpose in my letter of today of introducing an argument in it as to the legal situation of Formosa. You might, however, think over an argument that could be made; namely, that Formosa and the Pescadores are still in MacArthur's jurisdiction. The Japanese acquired them from China in 1895. In subsequent years, we frequently ratified the *status quo* of their possessions.

The Cairo Declaration and the Potsdam surrender were executive acts which were never matters of treaties ratified by the Senate. Such a ratification would only come up in a treaty with Japan, and MacArthur might collaterally hold them pending a treaty.

I enclose a note on these matters.

Yours faithfully,

HERBERT HOOVER

Honorable William F. Knowland
United States Senate
Washington, D.C.

NOTE ON FORMOSA

A. Background of Japan-Formosa relationship.

By the Treaty of Shimonoseki, signed April 17, 1895, by Japanese Count Ito and Li Hung-chang, Chinese Ambassador Extraordinary, China recognized the full independence of Korea and ceded to Japan the Pescadores, Formosa and the Liaotung Peninsula, paid an indemnity to Japan and negotiated a new commercial treaty.

Recognition took place, in effect, by the United States in the Root-Takahira Agreement of November 30, 1908, and the Lansing-Ishii Agreement of November 2, 1917. Both agreements proposed to "maintain the *status quo*," and by acquiescence, therefore, recognized Japan's position in Formosa.

B. Published documents of World War II do not mention Formosa until the Cairo Declaration.

(1) Cairo Declaration, December 1, 1943:

. . . Japan shall be stripped of all the islands in the Pacific which she has seized or occupied since the beginning of the first World War in 1914, and . . . all the territories Japan has stolen from the Chinese, such as Manchuria, Formosa, and the Pescadores, shall be restored to the Republic of China . . .

(2) Formosa was not mentioned in the official Protocol of Teheran or Yalta.

(3) Potsdam Ultimatum, July 26, 1945:

Point 8.
The terms of the Cairo Declaration shall be carried out and Japanese sovereignty shall be limited to the islands of Honshu, Hokkaido, Kyushu, Shikoku and such minor islands as we determine.

(4) Statement of White House on Occupation Policy in Japan, September 22, 1945:

. . . Japan's sovereignty will be limited to the islands of Honshu, Hokkaido, Kyushu, Shikoku and such minor outlying islands as may be determined, in accordance with the Cairo Declaration and other agreements to which the United States is or may be a party.

C. Geographic and ethnic makeup of Formosa:

(1) Off the southeast coast of China, the island has an area of about 14,000 square miles.

(2) Population in 1940 was 6,000,000; of which 91.5 percent were Formosan Chinese; 6 percent were Japanese; and 2.5 percent were aborigines.

On the Formosan Situation

Memorandum for an Editor

[January 29, 1950]

THE FORMOSAN situation seems now to have reached a center of utter confusion.

In December, according to eminent military authorities Formosa was vital to our Asiatic front against the tide of Communism. On December 23, the State Department deprecated its military importance. It was said, on January 5, that no military assistance would be sent. Yet, on January 23, it is announced that military supplies would be sent Chiang Kaishek from unexpended Congressional appropriations.

On January 26, according to Senator Connally and other reporters of the Foreign Relations Committee sessions, our military authorities considered Formosa "of strategic significance to the United States in the hands of an enemy." All which seems to leave open two questions:

1. What are we really going to do to prevent the island from falling into "enemy hands" if the appropriations are not enough?

2. Are we going to recognize Communist China and thus assume the Communists are not "enemy hands"? Or are we going to refuse recognition and support the integrity of Formosa? If so, how are we going to do it?

As to recognition, we might bear in mind that in eleven years —from 1933 to 1944—we either "recognized" or acquiesced in the annexation of some fourteen nations made Communist. From the first day to this we have had nothing from any of them but attacks, defamation of our country, conspiracies against our internal order, and opposition to every effort to bring peace to the world, except for the period when we furnished $10 billions of supplies to the Soviets. They do not seem to be "friendly hands."

There is also another confusing question: What rights have the people of Formosa?

Under all our promises from the Atlantic Charter down, we have insisted upon certain rights of self-determination and freedom of peoples. Formosa has only about 15 percent less people than Greece and at one time had maintained its independence. We insisted upon, and supervised, a free and unfettered election on whether the Greeks wanted a Communist government. We furnished vast military supplies, large military commissions to advise their resistance to Communist invasion from without.

I assume all defenses against Communist expansion are "calculated risks" of American boys. In the "calculated risks" we have already taken, we could include the Atlantic pact, the armament of Europe, the action in Greece, and the support of arms to Turkey. We also have about 150,000 boys on the Asian front and probably another 100,000 on the European front, in each case being more than merely forces to maintain order. How "calculated risks" are calculated seems confusing.

On Recognition of Communist China

Letter to Senator William F. Knowland, Washington, D.C.
[May 6, 1950]

New York, New York
May 6, 1950

The Honorable William F. Knowland
United States Senate
Washington, D.C.

My dear Senator:

You ask my view of the request you and your colleagues have made for a positive declaration that the United States will not recognize Communist China and that it will oppose its membership in the United Nations.

I do not assume there is any such intention but it is certain that such a declaration would clear up some of the fog in these questions.

Certainly the recognition of the Moscow satellite government in China would be a further surrender in the cold war which General Bradley intimates we are losing. It would be a further acceptance of the sweep of the Kremlin's aggressive militarism, agnosticism and Red imperialism. It is a system of immorality and without compassion that we cannot accept. It would plant another nest of Communist propagandists and agents in Washington and in every Chinese consulate over the land. It would betray millions of Chinese still struggling against a slave state.

The admission of Communist China into the United Nations with the support of the United States would inevitably result in all of the above effects. In addition it would add further to the already dominantly destructive forces in the United States.

If the United Nations is ever to be useful to the human race it must free itself of Communist domination—not add to it.

Yours faithfully,

HERBERT HOOVER

On the Committee for the Marshall Plan to Aid European Recovery

Letter to the Honorable Robert P. Patterson,
New York City
[February 9, 1948]

The following refers to a statement on the Marshall Plan
given on pages 120–130 in "Addresses upon the
American Road, 1945–1948":

New York, New York
February 9, 1948

The Honorable Robert P. Patterson
537 Fifth Avenue
New York 17, New York

My dear Mr. Secretary:

Upon my return from Florida, my attention has been called to the press release of your Committee in reply to a statement of mine upon the Marshall Plan.

I had made some recommendations based upon the considerable experience as to how the 6.8 billion dollars worth of commodities listed by the State Department from the Western Hemisphere (less some now confirmed unavailable commodities) could, by different methods of finance, be delivered during the first 15 months' period with a three billion dollar less cost to the American taxpayer. I suggested that an independent administration was essential and that no moral commitment be taken until proof had been given in this first period that the

86

promises of economic and military unity of Western Europe and its increased productivity were demonstrated.

Whether these suggestions met with your Committee's approval or not, it is at least unusual that such a responsible group of men should have given as an answer a brazen lie-smear that smacks of totalitarian intimidation of proper debate. You say: (*The New York Times*, January 25, 1948)

. . . that Mr. Hoover greatly underestimates the size of the world's economic problems today, as he did in 1946 when, as chairman of the Emergency Food Committee, he expressed the opinion that the food emergency should be over by the end of that summer. Unhappily, that emergency is still with us.

In the spring of 1946, I did serve in the then terrible world food crisis. In order to maintain hope and courage among eight hundred million hungry people, I stated that with the arrival of the 1946 harvest the worst would be over and that things would improve. It was based upon forecasts of agricultural authorities over the world. It proved correct. The food year which followed the 1946 harvest proved the best since the war. During that year rations were increased all over the world and no measures of American conservation of food were undertaken or were necessary, as there was no threat of mass starvation anywhere from lack of supplies. A far worse situation developed in the harvest of 1947, as to which I was the first to warn that conservation should be undertaken in the United States if the world was to have food this year.

I do not believe that this press release came from you, especially in view of the letters of high commendation which I received at that time for a successful service from you and other members of your Committee.

It would seem that a public rectification of this statement of your Committee would be in order.

Yours faithfully,

HERBERT HOOVER

On Policies of the International Bank for Reconstruction and Development

Letter to Mr. John J. McCloy, President, International Bank for Reconstruction and Development, Washington, D.C.
[July 5, 1948]

New York, New York
July 5, 1948

Mr. John J. McCloy, President
International Bank for Reconstruction
   and Development
Washington 6, D.C.

Dear Mr. President:

As I explained to you, I will not be able to attend the annual meeting of the Advisory Council. I have some diffidence in complying with your request for my views upon the Bank's policies. You and the Bank's staff are far more competent to determine such matters.

Such views as I have are more in the nature of impressions rising out of the changing times—and of less help than I could wish.

1. It seems to me that events have abundantly proved the original concept of the Bank as a major world-war reconstruction agency, lending money on adequate security with assurance of repayment, was an illusion. The physical, material, and political destruction of the war proved so great that there is, in major war-torn areas, for many years to come, little security obtainable

and little possibility of repayment such as this institution must have.

2. With a few exceptions major finance of reconstruction in these areas must be gifts, whatever other name they may be called by. The sums involved are in such large proportion for vanishing consumption goods, and the total sums are so huge, that they cannot be repaid. For instance, the post-war advances from the United States will aggregate probably thirty-five billions of dollars. At least some parts of this are called "loans." Even assuming a large increase in productivity of these areas and a large increase in their exports, the United States could not use the loan part of these advances in imported goods of the kind these debtors produce. Nor would the political structures of the debtors permit the abstraction of such an amount of goods from their standards of living. Much the same thing applies to huge obligations between other countries, such as the British obligations to the dominions and to other Sterling Bloc countries which were incurred to carry on the war. If there are any Lend-lease obligations extant, they also obviously cannot be repaid for the same reason.

3. So long as these illusionary sums hang around the world's neck, many of them purporting to be loans, they effectively block the possibilities of sound credit operations in these areas.

4. It may be argued that even in the presence of these huge obligations it is possible to make loans for special reproductive purposes and that by agreement from the increment of production such advances can be repaid. There may be some such minor exceptions. There may be cases of credits for raw materials with contracts to receive an export portion for repayment. Or there may be some reproductive industrial enterprise whose productivity warrants loan, and some special exchange arrangement might be set up for repayment. With currencies in the present state such assurances would be doubtful.

Also, in these areas they will prefer relief, or where they must take loans they will prefer the Export-Import Bank, where the Congress apparently expects more risks to be taken.

Aside from these particular difficulties in extending credits to the major war-torn areas, there are the problems of trade deficits, unbalanced budgets, political instability, etc., which inhibit normal banking operations.

5. I therefore doubt that the World Bank can perform any but minor functions in the major E. R. P. countries for some time to come. If it is to be operated as a real bank and not as a relief agency, I suggest that it must exclude any but minor operations in countries (*a*) with vast relief and war obligations until these are settled in some fashion by which real security can be given, and (*b*) until freedom and real stability of exchange is established.

6. The question before the Council seems to be that of what service the World Bank may perform in the meantime. If these limitations are correct, then the field of the Bank for the present must be mostly the old neutrals and countries like those in Latin America and the Near East, which are not bogged down with huge war obligations or artificial exchange and not in need of relief.

If the Bank for the present particularizes in the limited fields I have mentioned, in my view it should confine itself mostly to loans to governments for improvements of transportation, communications and irrigation projects. If title and taxes were placed upon a secure basis in these areas, there will be ample private capital for legitimate business enterprise. If that is not done, there is no foundation for business by the World Bank.

7. I do not see how the support of American private investors in the Bank's securities could justifiedly be obtained for other than business such as is mentioned in Paragraph 6.

Again, however, I must add these are only personal views.

Yours faithfully,

HERBERT HOOVER

Where We Are Now

Broadcast from New York City
[October 19, 1950]

THIS IS a good time briefly to appraise our international situation and our foreign policies. After that appraisal I shall offer some suggestions.

If we take a broad retrospective view of American foreign policies over the years after 1933, we will find one outstanding feature. All that time American statesmanship became lost when it came to the borders of Communism. And the consequences of our wanderings still crowd in upon us.

We first entered this swamp of lost statesmanship when we recognized the Communist government in 1933. Four Presidents and five Secretaries of State—Democrats and Republicans alike—had refused to invite Communist representatives into this American home of free men. Those Americans knew that all Communists carried germs of conspiracy intended to turn America into a police state, to destroy all religious faiths, to overthrow the freedom of men and the independence of nations.

If you need any reminders of what they did to our hospitality, read again the repentant Communist confessions, the Congressional exposures, the pleas of self-incrimination and the convictions of traitors in our courts. These carriers of evil germs penetrated into high places of government. They influenced national policies at the highest levels.

I will not dwell at length upon our successive wanderings into these sinister borders of Communism. However, I may mention our tacit alliance with Soviet Russia in June, 1941, while Dictators Stalin and Hitler engaged in war of mutual exhaustion. Many of us protested that such an alliance would spread Communism over the earth. Beyond this, in the words of a profound student, Hanson Baldwin, "The great opportunity of the democracies for establishing a stable peace came on June 22, 1941, when Germany invaded Russia, but we muffed the chance."

I could recall the step-by-step acquiescences and appeasements of Soviet Russia after we entered the war. They were punctuated by agreements made in Moscow in October, 1943; Teheran, one month later; Yalta, in February, 1945; and Potsdam, in August that same year.

In net result we abandoned the principles of the Atlantic Charter and the freedoms of men. In the end, we acquiesced in actual Russian annexation of about 40,000,000 free people in Northeast Europe. We acquiesced in her envelopment of the governments of over 500 million people of 13 nations behind the Iron Curtain in Europe and in Asia. Every stage of our relations saw compromises, appeasement, and defeat of American ideals and purposes.

Due to the valor of our soldiers and the energies of our industries, we won military victory in the war. But we lost the peace trying to appease the Communists.

We have constantly ignored Lenin's teachings which have been publicly known for thirty years. He said:

As long as capitalism and socialism remain we cannot live in peace. In the end one or the other will triumph—a funeral requiem will be sung either over the Soviet Republic or over world capitalism . . .

We have to use any ruse, dodges, tricks, cunning, unlawful methods, concealment and veiling of the truth.

Every year Stalin vows his loyalties to Lenin's teaching. All these 17 years have confirmed these malignant policies.

If you want more evidence that these are the principles of Soviet Russia, just remember that within twelve years they have violated 36 solemn agreements with other nations. They have vetoed efforts toward peace in the United Nations 45 times.

They engineered the attack on Korea. And every day they engage in defamation of the American people.

There is a stern lesson for the American people from these 17 years of experience.

Every American who has tried to deal with them has come away with his face and hands smeared with red tar.

Every time our government has attempted to co-operate with them, we become involved in a morass of lost statesmanship.

OUR PROBLEM NOW

The immediate problem which now confronts us is: How can we reorganize our instrumentalities for peace so as to give the world renewed hope? How can we secure peace—even an uneasy peace?

SEVEN INDIVISIBLE APPRAISALS

Before I make some suggestions, we must coldly appraise the world situation in which we find ourselves.

1. Our great hope is the United Nations. For five years, with the one exception of the Korean action when the Russians were away on a blackmail strike, they have paralyzed that organization.

2. Nothing will stop Red military aggression except an effective organized phalanx of the non-Communist world which will freeze the ambitions of the Kremlin.

3. We are told by many military authorities that Stalin could put 175 mobilized combat divisions on the European front within 90 days. We are told they have 30,000 tanks, thousands of planes, and the Atom Bomb. We are told they have large reserve forces. We are told that the Iron Curtain States have large armies poised for action. We are told they have huge forces in North Asia equipped by Russia.

In contrast we are told that the European nations now in the North Atlantic Alliance do not have available to Europe more than 30 active combat divisions with some air and naval power, with which to meet this horde from behind the Iron Curtain. We are told that South Asia has but little military strength to oppose the Communists.

4. The industrial potential of the United States can be over-powering in the long run. But Stalin, now having also the industrial power of the Iron Curtain States, can arbitrarily concentrate it on preparedness. Western Europe with a larger population than the United States has as large or greater industrial power than that of Stalin. It is being little occupied in preparedness. It could be quickly mobilized and could constitute a doubly overwhelming balance of industrial power.

5. We must realize, and the world must realize, that 160,-000,000 Americans cannot alone maintain the safety of the world against 800,000,000 Communists on the fronts of both Europe and Asia. Nor can we, out of our resources and manpower, contribute more than a minority part in such a phalanx of force.

6. We are told by the civilian and military leaders of our Government that we stand in the greatest of perils. We have inaugurated an immense military program.

The consequences of this program to our economic life are already evident. Under it taxes will take a greater portion of our national income than that taken by most non-Communist countries in Europe. Already we are in the midst of a disastrous wave of inflation from its pressures. We must defer many needed improvements.

We can stand this for possibly two or three years pending a genuine rally by the non-Communist world to its full part in defense. But we must in time have relief from a large part of that burden. We cannot carry the load for long without fulfilling Stalin's hopes of bleeding us economically to impotence.

7. There are three sources from which real military defense must come:

First. The European nations in the North Atlantic Alliance.

Second. The other non-Communist nations who are members of the United Nations, such as Canada, Latin America, the

Middle East, South Africa, Australia, New Zealand, and some of the smaller South Asian countries.

Third. And there is the United States.

THE DEFENSE OF WESTERN EUROPE

We will successfully clean up the Korean aggression under General MacArthur's brilliant generalship and teach a lesson.

However our greatest danger point to all Western Civilization is Western Europe. It is obvious, with the threats in Asia, that the United States can supply only a minor part of this huge European deficiency even with our present program.

The time has therefore come to speak frankly what is in the mind of many Americans today. And I speak not only as one who has witnessed two world wars, but with substantial military advice.

We know that the European nations now in the North Atlantic Pact (with American aid) have reached a greater industrial productivity than they had before either the First or Second World War. They have larger populations and more manpower than in those wars. In both those two wars, these peoples put in the field in 90 days over 140 equipped and trained combat divisions in addition to naval and air forces.

When the fabulous expenditures of various loans, together with the Marshall Plan and the North Atlantic Pact, were laid before the American people, certain results were promised. It was emphasized that besides economic and social objectives these gigantic sums would build the European nations into a united military defense against aggression upon Western Civilization. It was represented as the American first line of defense.

We consented to these sacrifices primarily on this promise. It has been costly. Outside of Lend-Lease during the war, we have spent, since the war ended, in gifts and loans (which are also bound to be gifts) almost 20 billions in Europe on this faith. We have not begrudged these huge sacrifices. But the result has been deeply disappointing to a growing body of Americans.

Competent observers are daily raising the serious question as to whether these nations, outside of Britain, have the will to fight, or even the will to preparedness. The actions and statements of their own leaders give little evidence of any real determination. In confirmation, I need only to quote Winston Churchill who stated, in a public address, a few weeks ago:

Imposing conferences have been held between military chiefs and experts, and a pretentious façade has been displayed by the governments responsible for our safety.

In fact, however, apart from the establishment of the American bomber base in England, nothing has been done to give any effective protection to our peoples from being subjugated or destroyed by the Russian Communist armies with their masses of armor and aircraft. I and others have given what warnings we could, but, as in the past, they fell on unheeding ears or were used to sustain the false accusation of warmongering.

Mr. Churchill seemed to think Europe had only two years in which to arm.

Our American officials in the recent conference of Foreign Ministers again urged the necessity of a unified European defense army embracing German components. That proposal has again been defeated or delayed.

All this situation has come as a great shock to thinking Americans. These failures raise serious questions. Are we being misled as to the seriousness of this situation? Have these nations such convincing evidence of the Kremlin's good intentions that they are not interested in defense? Has Karl Marx paralyzed the will of nations for independence? Do they expect the United States and Britain to carry the whole load in case of attack?

The time has come when the American people should speak out in much stronger tones than the diplomatic phrases of conference halls.

We should be willing to aid but, if Western Europe wants defense from the Communist tide, they must do most of it themselves—and do it fast.

Someone proposed that we at once increase our forces in

Europe to 10 combat divisions. That would be only a slaughter of American boys unless many times that number were standing by their sides.

We should say, and at once, that we shall provide no more money until a definitely unified and sufficient European army is in sight. And further that 10 American divisions will not be landed until then.

REORGANIZATION OF THE UNITED NATIONS

Nor is such an army in Europe even with American forces alone sufficient to dull Kremlin ambitions in both Europe and Asia.

Five months ago, and again three months ago, I urged that the United Nations be so reorganized as to permit the mobilization of the non-Communist world on military, economic, and moral bases to meet these aggressions. I suggested this could never happen with the Communists constantly making the United Nations impotent. I gave ample reasons.

The official reception of that idea was hostile. The press reception was sympathetic or favorable.

Every day since that statement was made has proved its validity. And the validity of that proposal was doubly proved three months ago when, for the first time in all its history due to the absence of the Communists, the UN has shown what real leadership could accomplish.

I have been gratified by the recognition of the validity of my suggestion by the proposals of a change in the rules of the UN by which Russian obstruction within that organization might be defeated.

MILITARY ORGANIZATION OF NON-COMMUNIST MEMBERS

Chapter VII of the United Nations Charter is a specific agreement as to mobilization of effective military and economic forces from every member to stop aggression. It provides in detail for its organization and command. For five years, the Russians have thwarted any practical realization of that agreement.

I am glad to see the recent proposals for the better mobilization of military strength by the members of the United Nations to stop aggression. That was also a step in the right direction.

However we must face reality. The United States ultimately must have relief from a considerable part of our present burdens. No patrols or token forces will present so grim a visage to Moscow as would choke their military ambitions.

We need strong medicine in the shape of large and definite armies both from European members of the North Atlantic Pact and from the other non-Communist members of the UN.

A METHOD OF RESOLUTE ACTION

To get action, either the potency and organization of the United Nations under Chapter VII should be so restored, notwithstanding Russian obstruction, as to take over a real job, or, alternatively, we should enlarge the North Atlantic Alliance into a world alliance which could in this fashion execute Chapter VII of the Charter.

We should, in either case, ask all nations who want to stop Russian aggression once and for all to join and to specify what they will join with and when.

We should say at once that the United States, with all its resources, cannot long endure the present drain on our economy. And if that fails, the world goes into night.

But if we do not find real military action of powerful strength in Western Europe, if there is no definite and effective mobilization of the other members of the United Nations so as to take up the major burden of their own defenses, then we had better reconsider our whole relation to the problem. In that event, we had better quit talking and paying, and consider holding the Atlantic Ocean with Britain (if they wish) as one frontier, and the Pacific Ocean with an armed Japan and other islands as the other frontier.

IN CONCLUSION

Let there be no misunderstandings.

I am conveying no military secrets to the Kremlin. They are able to read the open books of the democracies from our Congressional debates and our press even if they have no other intelligence service.

I am giving no aid to Stalin by stimulating defense against him.

I am not talking of any such thing as attack or a preventive war. I abhor the thought of it.

What I propose is such defense as prevents attack upon us.

I advise no retreat from the Communist front. I vastly prefer a consolidated front in full strength rather than being forced to reform our lines by failure of other nations.

What we want is real peace. But if we cannot have that, at least we want an uneasy peace within the economic burdens which the United States can bear.

Our hope must be that the Russian people will sometime, in perhaps the long future, throw off this evil regime as they did that of the Czars. Then real peace could come, because the mass of Russian people themselves are a peaceful people. With faith in God, that I believe will sometime be the outcome.

When Disarmament Can Come

Address in Response to the Presentation by General
Dwight Eisenhower of the First Award of the
Military Order of Foreign Wars of the
United States for Outstanding
Citizenship, New York City
[November 1, 1950]

I AM greatly honored by your Award. It will occupy a place among my family household gods. As that collection also contains various brickbats, this Award will serve a double purpose in military terms to "neutralize them in force."

President Truman recently sounded again the note of disarmament. That is a great ideal. It has been the aspiration of all good men for generations.

That aspiration was expressed in the Sermon on the Mount. It was one of the major purposes of the fifty nations who, out of the horrors of the First World War, signed the Covenant of the League of Nations. It was a major purpose of the nations who, out of the horrors of the Second World War, signed the Charter of the United Nations. Today in this distracted world, if a "free and unfettered" vote could be taken of the whole earth, I am sure an overwhelming number would vote for it.

But before I shortly discuss the problems involved, I give you an axiom.

Disarmament flows only from peace, not peace from disarmament.

To indicate some of these problems even in a world of peace and good will, I will recall to you some recent history. Peace was signed by all combatant nations after the First World War. For about thirteen years thereafter the face of the world was turned toward peace. There were no threatening military aggressors then discovered who disturbed men's sleep. During that period men of good will in the leadership of the free world charged themselves with disarmament.

The American Government called the Naval Conference of 1922. I served in that Conference. We brought about a reduction in battleships and aircraft carriers and established certain ratios of strength between the Great Powers. Later, when President, I secured a second Naval Conference in January 1930. It resulted in similar action as to cruisers, destroyers, and submarines which ended competitive naval building.

But we were not able to do more because peoples dependent for their very lives upon overseas supplies would not surrender their ability to protect their life lines. Other nations insisted upon maintaining naval strength in case the life-line saviors became aggressive against them.

During these same years the League of Nations was constant in its efforts to find a solution to land disarmament. Many commissions were appointed and many uniformly oratorical conferences were convened. These conferences rejected all such plans that amounted to total disarmament by overwhelming majorities; and they failed to agree on any intermediate steps.

America had already reduced her armies to a number less than our policemen. We had little to reduce. Yet during my Presidency, our Government joined in the last of those conferences, although we were not a member of the League.

After months of this conference, as they were not getting beyond the oratorical stage, I sent a message to them saying that "The time has come when we should cut through the brush and adopt some broad and definite method of reducing the overwhelming burden of armament which now lies upon the back of the toilers of the world."

I proposed a program, the nub of which was to reduce the power of the offensive, and thus increase the power of defense and thereby insure greater protection from aggression. To do this, I proposed we abolish the major instruments of aggressive warfare of that day, such as tanks, bombing airplanes, large mobile guns, and chemical warfare. I proposed also a basis for relative reduction of the size of armies, and a gradual reduction of war vessels, especially submarines. I said: "It is folly for the world to go on breaking its back over military expenditures. Nothing would create more hope in humanity than a start on such a program."

The suggestions were referred to a subcommittee of the League comprised of representatives of the General Staffs of all the member nations. To my utter surprise these soldiers voted—as I recollect—51 out of 54 in favor of these proposals. Many of the political leaders were enthusiastic but decision was deferred for more study and working out of detail.

In the meantime Mr. Roosevelt became President and he, too, adopted my proposals and urged the abolition of these weapons of aggression. But Hitler, Tojo, and Stalin then arose to threaten the world and all will to disarm was asphyxiated.

I recite all this for two purposes: First, as an indication that disarmament in any event could only follow a world of peace free from cold and hot wars; and second, to point out that even then disarmament can come only by difficult and slow steps.

However, I might indulge in purely mental exercise in stating how I would revise these proposals of years ago in the light of new events.

First. That we include the atomic bomb and guided missiles in the weapons of aggression.

Second. That the construction of surface naval vessels be halted—and that submarines be abolished.

Third. That independent commissions be established permanently in every country to see that these agreements are carried out.

Fourth. That as many of the aggressive weapons as the United Nations organization wants should be turned over for the exclusive use by that organization. Thus they could stop aggression in its tracks.

But when we look over the world today, any such steps are now absolutely unreal. I do not have the slightest faith that the militant Communism of Soviet Russia would accept them. Peace and good will are not in their hearts.

Therefore I do not depart from the statement I have made many times, that nothing will stiffle the Kremlin's aggressive ambitions except such organized military, economic, and moral force of all non-Communist nations as will confront the Politburo with the grim visage of defeat if they attack.

I am glad to see the preliminary steps now being taken by the Ministers of Defense in organization of a central command of the forces of the North Atlantic Pact nations.

Two weeks ago I stated that many thinking Americans were deeply disappointed and even shocked at the lack of interest or progress by the non-Communist nations to prepare for their own defense. I stated that the United States alone not only cannot defend them, nor can it long endure the economic strains of the military programs proposed to us. I said that unless we could quickly see far more action, we would need to re-form our American lines to a much restricted area which we could defend within our resources.

I can now amend that statement. Instead of using the words "many thinking Americans," I am now convinced I could have used the words "the majority of thinking Americans." I reach that conclusion from the editorial response to that address of two weeks ago. Measured in circulation or in numbers, a very large majority of the press editorials support the view I presented.

Perhaps this information would aid the Defense Ministers now in session in Washington and the representatives of other non-Communist countries in session at the United Nations. It might support them with their peoples at home if they knew this reaction of American opinion as to that address of two weeks ago.

However, the real solution of the world's greatest trouble would be for Soviet Russia to co-operate in promoting the welfare of mankind. They could join in a constructive peace with Germany, Austria, and Japan. Only by such a peace could steps be taken toward disarmament. Certainly the rest of the world would agree to join them in these objectives.

It is for this that we must pray to the Almighty.

PART III

REORGANIZATION OF
THE GOVERNMENT

Preface to "The Hoover Commission Report"

[McGraw-Hill Book Company, Inc., New York, 1949]

[EDITOR'S NOTE: *The reports of the Commission on Organization of the Executive Branch of the Government are too voluminous to be reproduced here. They have been published by the Superintendent of Documents, Washington, D.C., and also condensed into a single volume by the McGraw-Hill Book Company, Inc. Two whole volumes of analyses and presentation have been made by Bradley Nash and Cornelius Lynde,* A Hook in Leviathan, *and by Frank Gervasi,* Big Government. *The Introduction to the McGraw-Hill condensation was approved by Mr. Hoover and is produced here as descriptive of the work.*]

The reader may wisely bear in mind two factors which distinguish this book. First, few Government reports are "best sellers." Second, few attempts to reorganize the Federal Government have greatly excited public interest. Yet this report, in a far less manageable form, has already had wide circulation. It is believed that this is due to a public demand for information about Government reorganization that is without precedent.

Now for a guess at the reasons. It is worth noting that the unofficially famous "Hoover Commission" was officially christened, by the Congress which created it, "The Commission on Organization of the Executive Branch of the Government." Observe that this avoids the commonly used term, "reorganization," and hews to the real point which seems to be this: The Executive Branch has *never* been organized.

Here we speak of "organization" in common-sense business terms. The Government was not organized in George Washington's day nor was it in the time of Andrew Jackson. This worried Jackson and he tried to do something about it. Most Presidents have worried and tried since then. Among them were Presidents Taft, Wilson, Hoover, Roosevelt, and Truman. In turn they attempted to solve the problem by means of commissions, executive orders, and legislation. All met with scant success.

The Executive Branch under Mr. Hoover cost $4 billion a year to operate, and employed 600,000 persons. Lacking proper organization, it laid, even then, a great burden upon the Executive. Today, it requires an annual budget of $42 billion and employs 2,100,000 persons in an intricate structure of 1,816 assorted departments, bureaus, sections, divisions, administrations, etc. Manifestly no mere mortal President can carry the responsibility for personal direction of this establishment and have any time left for the broader duties of his office. What he cannot delegate officially he is forced either to delegate unofficially or neglect completely. The result, in either instance, is bound to be just what we have—duplication, overlapping, and administrative turmoil. We may have come at last to the point where officials and legislators will agree that "something must be done."

More importantly, the average citizen has become uncomfortably conscious of the vast size of our Government. We all want and expect many services from the Government, to be sure; but we are baffled by its magnitude, puzzled by its complexities, and frightened by its cost. Instinctively we see a possible danger to democracy itself.

Probably we, as citizens, have been looking unconsciously for something like the Hoover Commission Report, something that promises us a chance to see and understand the Government in Town Hall terms. If that is the case, it was no accident that the creation of the Commission and the publication of its report made national news from the start.

Most readers know the history of the Commission. It was created by unanimous vote of the Congress in July, 1947. The Lodge-Brown Act, which brought it into being, conceived of its mission on the highest possible plane. The Commission was bipartisan, with six members from each party. Four Commissioners each were chosen by the President of the Senate, the Speaker of the House of Representatives, and President Truman.

The choice of Mr. Hoover as Chairman was of course inspired. Always rated among the ablest administrators of all times, he alone, among living Americans, knows intimately the real problems which confront President Truman. Moreover, few men in our or any other day are so well qualified to execute a massive assignment in research. Many scholars still treasure his monumental reports on *Recent Economic Changes* and *Recent Social Trends* which this company had the privilege of publishing some years ago.

The Hoover Commission made a characteristically thorough and thoughtful approach to its mighty task. It began by defining some 24 of the principal problems of government and management. These included such things as personnel, budgeting and accounting, the Post Office, the National Security Organization, the State Department, and many other matters bearing on the assignment.

Having thus cut its cloth, the Commission created special research committees, called "task forces." These comprised some of the most eminent specialists available in each field. The task forces were given time, opportunity, and staffs with which to pursue their inquiries until they got to the general heart of each problem. Then, after periods of 10 to 14 months, they returned to the Commission with their findings in each field.

The result was the most imposing collection of facts, figures, and opinions on Government that has ever been assembled. It amounted, in fact, to some 2,500,000 words of basic data of the most valuable sort.

From this massive bulk the Commission then prepared to carve out the model of a streamlined, modern Government. For several months the Commissioners met at least three days each week. Taking each of the task force reports in turn, they selected the material of greatest value, considered all component parts with care, and brought them into an integrated whole.

To put it another way, Herbert Hoover and associates, as consulting engineers, have presented the American people with a blueprint for good government. In one sense it is the sort of report that an alarmed board of directors would hasten to obtain for the salvation of a rickety business. On a business basis alone, the Hoover Commission Report promises cash savings which have been estimated at more than $3 billions a year.

In human terms, the report has greater significance than any price tag can impart. As a people, we have reached the point at which the size and cost of government can easily impair the effectiveness of our economy, lower our standards of living, and weaken our effort to lead the free peoples of the world to safety from the encroachment of totalitarianism.

Mr. Hoover himself has put it this way: "Our field of inquiry not only concerns every citizen, it concerns the very strength and vitality of democracy itself. The success of this mission may well set the pattern for future joint participation by private citizens and Government representatives on matters affecting national welfare."

This volume is printed as a tool for the use of citizens, legislators, and Government officials in what may well prove to be— the times and the new attitude of the public considered — a genuine forward move in the direction of lasting good government. Certainly it is generally realized that fundamental reform of the Executive Branch is not the work of a moment. Suppose citizens and officials were to determine unanimously to put the Hoover report into effect at the earliest possible date. Even then the sheer mechanics of readjusting the huge and cumbersome governmental machine would take years to evolve. Meanwhile, a convenient reference work will be needed by all those who participate in the task.

We hope this book will help in that task. It presents the essence of the Commission's findings. Plucked from the heart of a vast body of task force research, it has also been stripped of the dissents, additional comments, and minority views of the various Commissioners. Note well that some of these reports were unanimously arrived at, while others were not. It would be strange, indeed, if 12 able men of diverse background and experience were to agree unanimously on all points of a program so vast and so varied. The Commissioners disagreed quite frequently. The dissents were fairly numerous and they had, like Supreme Court dissents, real value as commentaries on the problem.

There is a necessity, however, for a single volume which quickly answers the question: "What did the majority of the Commission determine?" It is to meet this need that we present this volume. We hope it may prove useful to those who work to make a lasting reality of this design for a Government which will forever be the servant, not the master, of our people.

THE PUBLISHERS

Policy Statement of the Commission on Organization of the Executive Branch of the Government

[Adopted on October 20, 1947]

THE reorganization of the government can be approached from three points of view: First, the necessity or desirability of a given function of the government; second, the exploration of the most advantageous structure of arrangement of these functions; and third, the improvement of its management.

There are certain obvious functions which need not be enumerated which are primary in government. There are certain functions which are useful in the development of national life and in the preservation of national ideals. But in all functions, there is the question of priority within national ability to pay. There are still further questions as to boundaries of federal versus state and local functions which jeopardize local government; and there are boundaries in functions by the overstepping of which government begins to stultify the initiative and productivity of the people.

The questions concerning structure largely revolve around consolidation of the activities of similar major purpose under one direction in order to prevent the waste, overlap, duplication and to secure unity and formulation and co-ordination of policies. In this same field of structure there are large problems created by failure in the past to pay full regard to the separation of legis-

lative, executive and judicial powers; there has been much trans-
gression over our fundamental concept of single-headed responsibility in administrative agencies and joint responsibility of
several minds in legislative or judicial agencies.

Assuming proper definition of function and proper structure,
the efficiency of internal management becomes the measure of
economy or waste in government.

Public Law 162 creating this Commission states that the purpose of the Commission is to study and determine and recommend what changes are necessary in the Executive to promote
economy, efficiency, and improved services in the transaction of
the public business by:

1. Limiting expenditures to the lowest amount consistent
   with the efficient performance of the essential services,
   activities, and functions;
2. Eliminating duplication and overlapping of services, activities, and functions;
3. Consolidating services, activities, and functions of a similar nature;
4. Abolishing services, activities, and functions not necessary
   to the efficient conduct of government, and
5. Defining and limiting executive functions, services, and
   activities.

Thus it is clear that the Commission is not confined to recom-
mending management or structural changes which improve the
efficiency of performance of the executive branch but is clearly
directed to exploring the boundaries of government functions
in the light of their cost, their usefulness, their limitations, and
their curtailment or elimination.

At various times over 40 years, commissions of investigation
and recommendation have been appointed by the Congress and
by the President. A mass of effectual information has been secured. At times a limited authority has been given by the Congress to the Executive to act in this field. Useful results have
been accomplished by the Congress and the Executive even with
the limitations of powers that have been given. A perusal of

these reports and of the actions taken in this field indicates that the major consideration has been given to structural changes. In no case has there been such a breadth of authority and instruction for so thorough an examination and recommendation as has been given under this law.

As a matter of fact, at no time has there been such a public desire for a complete reconsideration of the province of the Federal government and overhaul of the business methods of Federal administration and their relationship to the citizen. The need is much greater than at any time in the past. The huge expansion of the executive branch during the past 20 years has been made in an atmosphere of hurry and emergency which now calls for calm challenge.

COMMISSION PROCEDURE

It is imperative that the Commission make a fresh and more vigorous approach to the problem assigned to it than has hitherto been made.

For such a program it is proposed that the Commission should:

1. Denominate (for the purposes of its work) the principal groups of major-purpose activities and such functional problems as may extend over such groups.

2. Determine which of these groups or these functions should be taken up initially for consideration.

3. Enlist eminent and experienced citizens to explore and furnish the Commission with their steady judgment on what action should be taken in respect to each separate group or function. Such leaders would add public confidence to the conclusions of the Commission and would reduce the number of questions for final determination by the Commission. Each leader would need be free to organize his own task force to survey the particular functions assigned to them. They should be furnished with all existing material by the Commission's staff. Should they require further research, they should be authorized to secure their own research assistants.

4. This approach does not require much of an initial or an elaborate regular staff by the Commission, but rather a minimum staff which would co-ordinate and make available to these task forces the great mass of information now already accumulated by various parts of the government.

Memorandum on Task Forces
to Be Organized

[*October 20, 1947*]

T HE LAW of course requires that the Commission shall examine and report on all of the Executive departments and agencies in respect to the questions propounded by the Congress. If the work is to be divided into task forces, there may be ultimately 18 or 20 projects, and some determination is necessary as to the relative importance of these as a guide for the sequence of steps to be taken.

There are a number of investigations which are in progress which influence the question of priority in the Commission's work. For instance, the details of the consolidation of the Army and Navy are now being worked upon by the officials concerned, and until they have advanced in their work, the Commission should probably not wish to take any action. Under the Bureau of the Budget and the authority given by Congress, certain plans for structural reorganization are information for the action of the President. There are also the investigation and the plans in progress by the Comptroller General affecting budgetary and accounting methods and questions. Committees, both of Congress and the Department, are studying the overlap of federal and state taxation. It is proposed that the Commission should co-operate in these efforts or await further progress in them.

There is attached hereto a chart, based upon the one made by the Senate Committee on Expenditures in the Executive Departments, which gives the various agencies in detail, including the number of employees and approximate expenditures for the fiscal year 1947–48. On the basis of expenditures and employees, they would rank approximately as follows:

SUMMARY OF POTENTIAL EXPENDITURES FROM APPROPRIATIONS AND OTHER SOURCES, WITH NUMBER OF EMPLOYEES OF FEDERAL GOVERNMENT EXECUTIVE DEPARTMENTS AND AGENCIES

(Fiscal year 1947–48, listed in order of potential expenditure)

	No. of Employees	Millions of Dollars		
		Total Potential Expenditure	Appropriations	Other‡
1. National Defense	859,142	10,666	9,869	797
2. Veterans Administration	218,534	7,308	6,970	338
3. Treasury	95,294	1,875	1,800	75
4. Post Office	471,787	1,606	1,606	..
5. Agriculture	87,549	1,066	615	451
6. State	20,696	1,046	1,044	2
7. Federal Security Agency	34,405	1,023	911	112
8. Railroad Retirement Board	2,645	691	691	..
9. Atomic Energy Commission	4,105	425	175	250
10. Maritime Commission .	9,270	416	8	408
11. Emergency Agencies (7)*	51,114	350	350	..
12. Federal Works Agency.	24,547	340	336	4

‡ Other sources:
1. Administrative expenses authorized from operating or special funds
2. Prior appropriations
3. Authority to borrow (granted this fiscal year only, does not include previous authority granted but not utilized)
4. Contract authorizations

* Emergency agencies:
1. Joint Chiefs of Staff
2. Office of Defense Transportation
3. Office of Housing Expediter
4. Office of Scientific Research and Development
5. Philippine Alien Property Administration
6. Philippine War Damage Commission
7. War Assets Administration

	No. of Employees	Millions of Dollars		
		Total Potential Expenditure	Appropriations	Other‡
13. Civil Service Commission	3,408	263	263	..
14. Interior	52,813	245	204	41
15. Commerce	38,545	192	191	1
16. Justice	24,444	119	115	4
17. Labor	5,020	85	85	..
18. National Housing Agency	14,531	65	40	25
19. National Advisory Committee on Aeronautics	5,926	46	44	2
20. Regulatory Agencies (9)†	7,742	40	40	..
21. Reconstruction Finance Corporation	7,718	39	..	39
22. Tennessee Valley Authority	14,258	34	19	15
23. Panama Canal	25,556	21	21	..
24. Other Agencies (13)..	4,063	14	12	2
Total Executive Branch 2,084,188		27,974	25,412	2,562
Total Legislative Branch		93		
Total Judiciary		552		
District of Columbia		96		
Interest on Public Debt		5,000		
Payments to Government Trust Funds		414		
Total cost of Goverment 34,129				

(Excluding any future commitments for foreign aid in 1947–48)

† Regulatory agencies:

1. Civil Aeronautics Board
2. Federal Communications Commission
3. Federal Power Commission
4. Federal Trade Commission
5. Interstate Commerce Commission
6. National Labor Relations Board
7. Securities and Exchange Commission
8. U.S. Tariff Commission
9. Tax Court of U.S.

The pattern of these task forces is only in part departmental. They are mostly matters which concern several agencies. The Post Office is a good example of a departmental problem. It is an integral unit probably exercising no duplicating nor overlapping activities. It is therefore not affected by other structural changes in the government. There is probably very little question in the Post Office Department as to unnecessary functions or as to functions which encroach upon state or local government. The major question in the Post Office Department is management. To adequately examine this phase, a task force directed at the examination of the Department should be constituted of men who have had experience in some kind of comparable communications service.

Relative expenditures might indicate something of a comparative opportunity for economies, but they do not necessarily constitute the guide to the rotation of the Commission's task. More especially is this true because many of the problems before the Commission are problems of structure which apply to many different departments, and are problems of functional borders.

During the past years a great deal of the basis of complaint has been the presumed overlap and duplication among the different governmental agencies. Much of this has been remedied. It would seem desirable, however, to put on a task force of men acquainted with the Federal structure, to examine how far previous recommendations to remedy the overlap and duplication have been adopted and where there are glaring instances still outstanding. With the amount of data already in hand, this is not a very major task, but such action would clear a good deal of air.

This Congressional chart shows the Executive branch of the government as comprising the 10 major departments, 25 independent agencies, 9 regulatory bodies, and 7 emergency agencies. Every President has protested that it is absolutely impossible to administer so many agencies directly responsible to himself. One of the constant debates over 30 years has been the pro and con of establishing new departments of the government to gather in the independent agencies under better control. The problem involves consideration of the expansion of the number of Cabinet officers. The early determination of the Commission's judgment on these questions will affect many other structural questions. A much greater structural question lies in the relation of the President to the Executive and to other departments of the government.

FISCAL, BUDGETARY, ACCOUNTING METHODS, AND CONTROL

A task force directed at this question is of early importance to examine the whole fiscal, budgetary, accounting methods, and financial control of the government agencies. The successful efforts undertaken by the Comptroller General for uniform methods of budgeting and accounting should be supported by further exploration of the whole problem.

REGULATION OF COMMERCE AND INDUSTRY

The regulation of business to prevent oppression in a free economy is, of course, one of the primary functions of government. While the nine important regulatory commissions are not generally considered part of the Executive, inasmuch as a number of them do exert executive authority, their whole relationship to the Executive branch should be considered by this Commission.

Another problem in this connection is the quasi-judicial authority exercised by executive officials. In both cases there is insufficient supervision and great confusion of the three powers.

Moreover, the problem arises of the possible simplification of the relationship of these regulatory agencies with the public, which would greatly relieve some of the burdens upon the citizen.

PROTECTION OF CITIZENS AND ENFORCEMENT OF THE LAW

A large question arises as to what degree law enforcement should be concentrated in the Department of Justice or what the relations of the Department of Justice should be to the enforcement and protective functions of other agencies of the government.

DEFINITIONS OF FEDERAL VERSUS STATE FUNCTIONS

The whole borderline between federal and state governmental functions needs thorough review. There are probably more overlapping efforts and duplicating burdens on the citizen in this borderline field than there are internally in the Federal Executive establishment.

On the National Security

Statement before the Senate Armed Services Committee,
Washington, D.C.
[April 11, 1949]

1. I believe it is generally accepted that the National Security Act of 1947 was a great step in the direction of better national security organization. In many aspects, however, it has not entirely accomplished the high hopes of unity, economy, and civilian control which were expected. The failures and their causes are dealt with in detail in the Report of the Commission of which I have been Chairman, and by the Task Force which I appointed to make a detailed investigation of the subject.

The central weakness, as stated in the President's message, by the statement of Secretary Forrestal, and in the reports of both the Commission and the Task Force, lies in the lack of clear authority and responsibility assigned to the Secretary of Defense. The set-up under the Act of 1947 covered the establishment of seven main agencies: that is, the National Security Council, the National Security Resources Board, the Secretary of Defense, the Joint Chiefs of Staff, the Munitions Board, the War Council, and the Research and Development Board. The major function of all of them was to co-ordinate the policies and administration of the three great services of national defense. The deficiency in that set-up was the lack of a center point of clear administrative authority.

2. The proposed amendments in Section 4 of this Bill (S 1269), by providing for definite central administrative au-

thority in the Secretary of Defense, seek to cure that deficiency. These amendments should clarify this situation and are generally in accord with the recommendations of the Commission. I believe the change of name from the National Military Establishment to the Department of Defense in Section 3 is essential in order to establish the climate of budgeting, unity, and teamwork which is the underlying purpose of all this legislation.

The amendment in Section 2, by which the President obtains greater latitude in appointing members to the National Security Council, is constructive. The present Council, with four out of seven members from the military arms, is overweighted from that quarter. The provision in Section 5, for an Under Secretary of Defense, is necessary. I will comment later upon the provision for three Assistant Secretaries.

There is an important departure from the recommendations of our Commission, and there is, in my view, a vital omission in the Bill which I will discuss later.

3. The amendment in Section 6-*b*, providing for a chairman of the Joint Chiefs of Staff, is not in accord with the majority views of the Commission on Organization, or the Task Force, or with my own views. It is proposed that this chairman shall be the "principal military advisor to the President and the Secretary of Defense" and with rank higher than the other members of the Joint Chiefs of Staff. In my view this will in effect constitute him a single Chief of Staff. The majority of the Commission on Organization and the Task Force, after careful consideration and investigation, were opposed to this idea.

The majority of our Commission recommended that there be a chairman who would be a presiding officer to expedite the work of the Joint Chiefs, who would have no vote and no powers of decision, who would present the views of the Secretary of Defense to the Joint Chiefs, and who would report their views to the Secretary. Generally, it was our view that the Joint Chiefs should be the principal military advisors and that here was a case for combined judgment of the three arms, with final decision resting with the Secretary of Defense, or with the President, or the Congress, in the case of conflict. The objections to such a chairman as this Bill proposes are: that it places too much power in a military man; that it would lessen civilian control of the military arm; that the three Joint Chiefs of Staff would be removed, in effect, from their responsibility as chief advisors to the President and the Secretary of Defense; that any chairman would have to come from one of the Services, which would give that particular Service two votes in times of decisions. It is my belief that the proposed set-up would create all the liabilities and none of the assets of a single Chief of Staff and would produce wider disunity than before. We need unity in national policies, in strategy, and of command in action. But we also should preserve the identity of the three Services. This implies difficult border lines, but a chairman with the position and powers outlined in this Bill dangerously oversteps these boundaries.

4. The important omission in this proposed legislation, to which I have referred, lies in the area of the budget and accounting systems. On that subject, as Chairman of the Commission on Organization, I set up a special Task Force of most eminent accountants of wide government experience. Their experience, added to that of the Commission itself, has been laid before the Congress in our special Report on Budgeting and Accounting. Their task was to examine the budgeting and accounting in every part of the Executive Branch. In addition, however, I directed a combination of the Task Force on Defense and the Task Force on Budgeting and Accounting to investigate those questions in the Defense Establishment with special care. Their detailed report has not been printed, but I present it herewith to the Committee. Summaries of it appear in the printed reports. I commend the whole text to your most earnest attention. It displays a startling state of affairs.

This Report states:

The Committee feels that it is justified in saying that our military budget system has broken down. The budgetary and appropriation structures of the Army and Navy are antiquated. They represent an accumulation of categories arrived at on an empirical and historical basis. They do not permit ready comparisons, they impede administration, and interfere with the efficiency of the military establishment.

Congress allocates billions without accurate knowledge as to why they are necessary and what they are being used for.

The remedy lies not alone in the general provision of authority to the Secretary of Defense in this Bill, but amendment to various laws and provisions to cover the whole budgeting and accounting process. This reform should follow the principles stated in our Report on that subject which proposes a "performance" or functional budget, with modern and uniform accounting methods, the accounts to be kept in the Department.

No one can tell from the present budget what any particular function or activity costs. In our reports we give the Bethesda Hospital as a simple example of present budgeting methods in the Defense Establishment. The hospital receives allotments from 12 different appropriations and nowhere is its total cost shown. We also give an example of the "performance" budget, applied to the whole Navy Department.

I will not take time with details. But I would like to emphasize that radical reform of budgeting and accounting lies at the very root of economy in this Department. Without such reform, neither the President, nor the Department, nor the Congress, nor the public can understand what the expenditures really are and where economies can be applied.

I may mention that there are four forms of accounts in the Government—or there should be—the accounts of appropriations and funds, the fiscal accounts, property accounting, and cost and comparative accounting. The appropriations and funds accounts are kept outside the Department by the Comptroller General, who is the agent of Congress. The fiscal accounts are kept by the Treasury, and nobody keeps the property and cost and comparative accounts. The whole concept of appropriations accounts, kept outside of the Department, is the negation of any sound business practice. It disarms the administrative officials of the daily use of one of the primary implements of administration. Obviously the Comptroller General should approve any system of accounts installed and should audit these accounts.

5. An equally important reform is needed in the civilian

services in these Departments. In 1943, there were about 9,000,000 military men and about 2,000,000 civilians in the Military Establishment. A year ago, there were about 1,700,000 military men and 860,000 civilians in the Establishment. In other words, in the first instance there was one civilian for every four military men, and at present there is about one civilian for every two military men. There seems room for economy in this quarter.

It is hopeless for the Civil Service Commission to attempt to recruit the number of persons with 10,000 different skills which are required in this Department. The selection of civil servants should be delegated to the Department and its branches under rules to be established and enforced by the Civil Service Commission, which will secure selection on the basis of merit and free of politics. The whole basis of rating, promotion, and severance must be reformed if we are to secure an efficient and economical civil service.

6. I may now return to the question of the three Assistant Secretaries for the Secretary of Defense, which I referred to a moment ago. Objection has been raised to the title—Assistant Secretaries—as confusing with the Secretaries of the Army, the Navy, and the Air Force, and the danger that perhaps through their titles they would assume to supplant the administrative powers of the three major Secretaries. There is merit in this objection. This recommendation arose in the Commission on Organization out of our over-all recommendations for certain staff assistance to the Secretaries of all Departments. The Commission recommended a group of staff officers concerned with budgeting, accounting, procurement of supplies, personnel, management research, and publications, but having no administrative powers. Such staff officials are needed by the Secretaries of the Army, the Navy, and the Air Force. However, in the case of the Secretary of Defense, as outlined in this Bill, the Chairman of the Munitions Board would serve the procurement function. But the Secretary of Defense has need of officials to co-ordinate budgeting and accounting, personnel, public information and publications. Those functions were, at least to my mind, the

duties for which the three Assistant Secretaries were proposed. To avoid the conflict of titles, I suggest these officials be established and that they be given some title which would indicate their functions instead of the title of Assistant Secretaries. As I have said, they are not to be administrative officials, for operating functions rest in the Secretaries of the Army, the Navy, and the Air Force.

7. Something needs to be said as to economy in these Services. The military burden today, added to our other expenditures, is seriously imperiling the economy of the country. There are great savings to be made in the Department. And by savings I mean attaining the same ends for less expenditures. No one could estimate their amount. I requested the Chairman of the Task Force engaged in this investigation to estimate what the savings might be, if all the reforms proposed were adopted. His guess was $1 billion 500 millions annually in money or money's worth. You can reduce this estimate greatly and it still indicates a staggering waste. And it is a waste beyond the power of Congress or civilian officials to control under the present set-up.

THE COMMISSION on Organization of the Executive Branch of the Government, of which I have been chairman, urged legislation on the major lines of the Senate Bill (1843) which you are considering. In our Commission reports and that of our Task Force, we furnished exhaustive reasons and information upon which our recommendation is based. As this material is available to the members of the Committee, I will not repeat it here.

I believe it is generally agreed that the National Security Act of 1947 did not accomplish the high hopes of unity of command, civilian control of the financial and business operation of the military forces, and the economy that was expected of it, and that the central weakness lies in lack of clear authority and responsibility assigned to the Secretary of Defense.

I may well comment that legislation on the lines of the Senate Bill has been recommended by President Truman; the late Secretary of Defense, James Forrestal; the present Secretary of Defense, Louis A. Johnson; former Secretary of War, Robert P. Patterson; Secretary of Air, W. Stuart Symington; Ferdinand Eberstadt, Chairman of our Task Force, and many others familiar with the problem. There is added indication of the need for this legislation as it was unanimously approved by the Senate Committee on Armed Services and passed the Senate without a consequential dissent.

There are, of course, differences of view upon secondary

matters in this legislation, but, I believe, general agreement as to the weaknesses of the present organization and the major remedies.

BUDGETING, ACCOUNTING, AND AUDIT

In my statements to the Senate Committee on the Armed Services, I urged that much stronger provisions be made in the draft legislation then being considered for accounting, budgeting, and audit, and for the administration of these functions. There can be little start at real economy until these obsolete methods, especially outmoded by the growth of the Services, are reformed. Those recommendations have been worked out in Title IV by the members of the Senate Committee in co-operation with Mr. Eberstadt and the specialists of our Task Forces, who were engaged in the investigation of these questions, together with the Secretary of Defense and other departmental officials. I believe they are excellently formulated.

CHIEF OF STAFF

There is only one point of consequence where the Senate Bill departs from the recommendations of the majority of the Commission on Organization and the majority of our Task Force. That relates to the Chairman of the Joint Chiefs of Staff.

Our recommendations were that there be an independent chairman of the Joint Chiefs of Staff to serve as a presiding officer; to report decisions or disagreements to the Secretary of Defense, but to have no decisions, no vote or other authority.

The Senate Bill in Section 211, however, provided:

The person appointed as Chairman shall, while holding such office, take precedence over all other officers of the armed services, and shall receive the highest rate of pay and allowances prescribed by law for the Chief of Staff of the Army, the Chief of Naval Operations, or the Chief of Staff of the Air Force: Provided, That the Chairman shall not, by virtue of his office, exercise military command over the Joint Chiefs of Staff or the services.

and Section 211 also states:

(d) The Chairman of the Joint Chiefs of Staff as such shall act as the principal military adviser to the President and the Secretary of Defense and shall perform such other duties as the President and the Secretary of Defense may direct or as may be prescribed by law.

This, in my view, will in practice amount to the constitution of a single Chief of Staff, who will become the voice and leader of all the military forces. Our Commission and our Task Force gave long investigation and consideration to this question.

Our reasons against such a concept were that it places too much power in any military officer and thus checks the vital civilian control of the Armed Services; that with such rank and power his voice to the country can override the responsible civil officials; that such dominant influence would not foster economy; that the Joint Chiefs of Staff would, in effect, be rendered remote from their real responsibility as advisers to the Secretary of Defense and the President; that it unduly minimizes the separate functions of the three military arms, and limits unduly their separate identity; that such an arrangement gives two votes to one of the three services because the Chairman must be chosen from one of them; that such dual action and competition for the appointment among the services would produce disunity rather than unity. My belief is that this provision is not only unworkable, but dangerous to the country.

We need unity in strategy and unity of command in action. That should be the duty of the Joint Chiefs of Staff to bring about. If they fail, then the responsibility should rest on civilian control, first on the Secretary of Defense and, second, on the constitutional Commander-in-Chief of the Armed Forces, who is the President.

ECONOMIES

There is no doubt that great economies can be brought about by this legislation without lowering the efficiency of the defense arm. Any estimate must be speculative. Our Task Force placed them at a minimum of $1 . 5 billions annually. Secretary Symington used the expression "billions." Secretary Royall stated that with these powers a billion dollars could have been saved this year and, at the same time, provided better defense.

You can discount these figures considerably and find in them reasons for this legislation. It would give some relief to the acute economic strains, which are now evident as arising from the cost of government.

Statement before the Armed Services Committee,
House of Representatives,
Washington, D.C.
[October 21, 1949]

A T THE outset I wish three matters to be understood:
First, that I am here at the request of the Committee;
second, that I have no desire to add to the bitterness
which has already flooded out of this hearing; and third, that
the Committee will not expect me to resolve the technical question as to whether the B-36 can, or cannot, do everything that is
claimed for it. I presume, however, that I have been asked to
come for discussion of wider purposes than that.

SOME PUBLIC ASPECTS OF THESE HEARINGS

At the outset I should like to say something as to the public
aspects of these hearings. We need peace within the Armed
Services. We need it for morale and for the good of our national
defense.

It must be a matter of regret for our entire country and for
the nations of Western Europe that differences of view on these
questions have not been resolved within the walls of the military
services.

However, I suppose one of the requirements of maintaining
freedom is the public washing of linen. But an equal requirement is that we settle down afterwards to loyal co-operation and
constructive action.

The many men who have appeared here are really great public servants. They are all moved by earnest and even emotional

interest in our national defense. They are brave men used to speaking their minds, and we would not want them otherwise.

We must remember that the whole development of defense is a constant shift into new weapons and new methods of warfare, along with the new quarters from which our dangers may come. These shifts always create divisions of opinion and hot debate among the most skilled and the most earnest of men. During my administration we struggled out of the cavalry into mechanized divisions. Today air power is in increasing degree a factor in both land and sea power. As some weapons become less effective and others more effective, the life training of some officers in them is often a reason for their reluctance to alter them. On the other hand, equally earnest men wish to move too quickly into every new field, no matter how experimental. It is fortunate that we have both groups and men who will speak their minds.

Regrettable as some expressions in these hearings may have been, they will have served a purpose now that everybody has been given a chance to have his say—if we now have a renewed effort to make our defense into a team.

THE UNIFICATION ACT

It seems to me that the first interest of Congress is whether it has set up in the Armed Services Unification Act an effective method of determining such questions as are here discussed and the efficient management of our defense. The Act has been at least implicitly under attack in these hearings.

Yet it would scarcely seem necessary to defend an Act which has been so insistently demanded by the country, by experienced officials, and twice fully canvassed by the Congress. It was the outgrowth of lack of unity in command and huge waste in the last war followed by a continuing disunity and waste in peace.

Prior to the recent Unification Act, the Commission created by the Congress, of which I was Chairman, and its task force under Mr. Eberstadt reported that we found continued disharmony and lack of unified planning. We found that extravagance in military budgets and waste showed a lack of understanding of their effects upon our whole economy. We found that interservice rivalries indicated a lack of understanding that military security depends not upon equal appropriations to each service but upon their being pointed to the actual military situation in the world. We stated that there was a lack of central civilian authority over these services—that the divided authority and lack of allegiance to a common objective amounted to an almost complete absence of control. We recommended a form of organization that should solve these questions. I see nothing in these hearings that would change those recommendations.

The action by Congress to remedy these ills in my view represents one of the most constructive achievements by Congress. The mechanisms provided by that legislation establish methods for dealing with the very problems presented in your hearings. The last Act has been in operation less than four months. It requires a year for newly wedded couples to get used to each other.

The machinery set up to determine strategic plans, problems of command, and technical questions would seem to provide ample representation and every protection to the views of each of the services. Its machinery provides for a National Security Council, a National Security Resources Board, a Munitions Board, a Research and Development Board, a War Council, Secretaries for each arm of the service, a separate military staff in each service, and a Joint Chiefs of Staff to deal with such questions as the efficacy of the B-36, and for their aid, the Joint Staff, and the Weapons Systems Evaluation Group to prepare strategic plans. In all these agencies each of the three services is represented. I see no basis for complaint that adequate representation and adequate machinery to develop facts and conclusions have not been provided. I have no doubt that among these agencies there is the skill to settle technical and strategic and command questions.

If the services finally disagree, there is no alternative but the decision of the Commander-in-Chief through the Secretary of Defense. If the Commander-in-Chief goes wrong, the final decision must be with the Congress. I do not believe anyone has challenged the fundamental that in the last analysis there must, in our Republic, be civilian control of the military arm. This is not only an essential for reasons of state, but because ofttimes the military arms must have outside aid for inside reforms. No better instance of the need of civilian control is necessary than the fact that the total original budget for this year presented by the three services was seven billion dollars more than was presented to the Congress by the civilian Secretary of Defense.

RIGID ECONOMY IN THE CONDUCT
OF OUR ARMED SERVICES

One of the major purposes of the unification acts has been the elimination of duplication and waste in the three services. The creation by the Congress of the Commission on Organization of the Executive Branch was for the purpose, among others, of investigation of opportunities and recommendation of remedies in the Armed Services. I do not need to review those extensive recommendations which were the outcome of exhaustive investigation. They are already familiar to you. They extended over obvious fields, such as accounting, budgeting, personnel, duplication of transport, purchasing, recruiting, hospital facilities, etc. There was a general agreement by all agencies that a minimum of a billion dollars annually, and possibly two billions, could be saved without impairing the defense of our country.

To effect these things, someone must take the final responsibility. Secretary Johnson has put into action parts of these recommendations. They obviously raise criticism from those of fixed minds or from those who are disturbed. He deserves the full support of this Committee and the country in his difficult task.

One phase of this economy problem is the idea which has been advanced that administrative officers should spend the full appropriations of the Congress. This may well apply to some special desire of the Congress, but it should not be a general rule. Otherwise the whole purpose of Congressional legislation for economy, such as arose from our Commission's recommendations, is made futile.

THE PRESSURE ON OUR ECONOMY

I wish to emphasize the pressure on our economy. It is costing us, in one direction or another, almost $24 billions annually. Already we have a budget deficit in sight of $5 or $6 billions for this fiscal year and perhaps more next year. That can mean but one thing—inflation—which will damage every worker and every farmer in the United States. In my view, our productive economy is already so heavily taxed as to slow up progress in its improvement of methods and its necessary expansion to meet the demands of our increasing population. We cannot continue such burdens for long.

On Expenditures in the Executive Office

Statement before House Committee on Expenditures,
Washington, D.C.
[January 31, 1949]

THIS LEGISLATION is just the first, and a necessary
step, in the grievously needed reorganization of the
Executive Branch of the Government.

I need not point out that, first, we must get these 1,800
"Bureaus," "Commissions," "Divisions," "Departments," "Administrations," and offices into some sort of orderly relation
before we can even begin on the further steps which reorganization requires. That is the object of this legislation. There were
only about 350 of these "agencies" twenty years ago, and that
was too many even before the depression, and war multiplied
them about four times. To secure efficiency and economy in the
Government we must begin at this point to resolve them.

However, the most perfect alignment of these agencies would
not solve the whole problem of reorganization. Other vital
steps will also be necessary and will require different legislation.
That is because aside from multiplicity and overlap in these
agencies, their officials are, like Gulliver, enmeshed by thousands
of strands of red tape, accumulated by legislative and executive
action over half a century which paralyzes the efforts of the
best of them.

As to the first step proposed in this bill, it is hopeless to expect
Congress to investigate and legislate out the vast detail of the

overlaps, the conflicts, the duplications, and the lack of co-ordination among this multitude of agencies.

This is no creation of dictatorial powers. This bill proposes that the President take the initiative and propose plans for the redistribution of executive agencies to the Congress and that Congress reserve a veto power over such plans that he may propose. The sole purposes are to reduce expenses, gain efficiency, and make life easier for the citizen in his dealings with the Government.

REGULATORY AGENCIES

So far as I know, it is not proposed that the President should interfere with the quasi-judicial or quasi-legislative functions of the major "regulatory agencies," such as the Interstate Commerce Commission, the Federal Trade Commission and others.

I do not wish to be offering opinions on constitutional questions but I may say that it has been my own opinion that these "regulatory agencies" are not a part of the Executive Branch of the Government. They might thus be considered to be outside the constitutional mandate that "The executive power shall be vested in the President of the United States." The real problem is that these agencies thus being "independent" of the President's powers have branched out into purely executive functions. Prominent examples are the great business operations of the Maritime Commission and the railway safety inspection activities of the Interstate Commerce Commission. Assuming these "regulatory agencies" are independent of the President, it is a certainty that for orderly government their executive functions should be moved to the Executive Branch of the Government where they are within the authority and responsibility of the President. These administrative activities of the "regulatory agencies" may be a violation of the spirit of the Constitution and in any event, they are bad government. Their executive functions, as distinguished from their quasi-judicial and quasi-legislative functions, should be placed with functions of the same major purpose in the executive departments if we are to plane out overlaps and have a businesslike administration.

THE REASONS FOR THIS LEGISLATION

This first step in reorganization is an endeavor to solve two problems.

The first is to place, and at times consolidate, these 1,800 "agencies" into groups of major purpose. Many agencies of related purpose are scattered over the Government. Such ill-setting creates constant overlaps, conflicts of jurisdiction, competition, and waste. And perhaps worst of all, it prevents development of unified purpose and policies. They should be placed cheek by jowl with each other under some single head who can reduce them to order.

Just as instances, there are over 30 agencies engaged in lending money, making guarantees, or insurance activities. There are 23 agencies engaged in major construction activities competing with each other for labor and materials, and scattered over 11 departments or agencies. There are 10 agencies dealing with major transportation questions (not including regulatory functions) scattered through 8 departments and independent agencies.

Not all of such agencies can be set in one spot, but the situation can certainly be improved.

The second problem is to relieve the President of administrative detail and free him for more important duties of his office. I have here three lists of agencies (outside the regulatory agencies) that report direct to the President. One list shows 65 such agencies; another shows 94; and still another shows 101. The discrepancy in the lists is a difference of opinion as to how much responsibility the President has for them. Most of them exercise some executive function.

Of them, some 18 or 20 are major operational "departments," or "administrations," leaving somewhere between 45 and 80 secondary agencies reporting to the President—if they report to anyone. These agencies are usually, and significantly, referred to as the "independent agencies." If the President were to give each of them an hour a week, he would have no time for his major responsibilities in national policies and the conduct of the major "departments" and "administrations." In fact, the President cannot physically look after these "independent agencies" and they have little checking or direction. The idea is to place as many of them as possible under the direction of the major departments or administrations. My personal hope is that the total number of agencies of all kinds reporting to the President can be reduced to less than twenty.

SOME MINOR HISTORY

This legislation is not new.

After the failure of Presidents previous to my time to persuade Congress to remedy this problem of rearranging the agencies, I first recommended, in 1931, this idea of Presidential initiative in proposing plans with a Congressional veto. But the Congress of that time reversed the veto idea to a requirement of affirmative action by the Congress. That reduced the proposal to the level of any other general recommendation to the Congress. However, I sent to the Congress at that time proposals to combine 59 agencies into 9, out of the 350 then existing, but Congress took no affirmative action.

It was not until 1939 that Congress finally adopted this plan of action. Some progress was made under this authority to Presidents Roosevelt and Truman, although the powers to make such proposals were greatly restricted. In the meantime, due to war and other causes, the number of agencies in the government has grown hugely. The authority to the President to initiate reorganization programs expired last April.

In closing, I think it is appropriate for me to repeat a statement which I made to the Congress 17 years ago (February 17, 1932):

"We may frankly admit the practical difficulties of such reorganization. Not only do different factions of the Government fear such reorganization, but many associations and agencies throughout the country will be alarmed that the particular function to which they are devoted may in some fashion be curtailed. Proposals to the Congress of detailed plans for the reorganization of the many different bureaus and the independent agencies have always proved in the past to be a signal for the mobilization of opposition from all quarters which has destroyed the possibility of constructive action."

The Need for Reorganization

*Address before the Chamber of Commerce of
the State of New York, New York City
[March 3, 1949]*

YOUR CHAIRMAN suggested that you might like to know something about the work of the Reorganization Commission, and that I might devote a moment to it, although I know you are all busy people and would rather be elsewhere probably. In any event, that work has reached its final stage of reports, and its findings of recommendations to the Congress. They should all be public within the next month, and I will not review all of the facts and ideas that are presented there. I leave that as a part of your homework on civil government, I advise you to undertake it.

Today, there are bitter complaints from all over the land as to the size of the Federal bureaucracy. There are, in fact, more Federal officials in many states than there are combined state, municipal and county, including the police. In fact, I think there are more in the nation than the whole of the governmental employees otherwise, and that does not include the military.

These Federal employees have grown from 570,000 to about 2,200,000 in less than fifteen years, but they are not in Washington. Ninety percent of them are out in the sticks, endeavoring under direction from Washington to improve the lot of the citizen, whether he likes it or not. Often their energies are devoted to taking something away from him.

This Commission hopes that its work will serve to reduce

the number of these employees somewhat, but the cause of this growth lies far deeper than this Commission can remedy.

You may have a short explanation as to how we got this way, and I know what you would be likely to say and whom you would blame, but it is deeper than that. In addition to the natural instinct of bureaus to exfoliate in their desire to improve the lot of man, there are two great pressures that are at work in our country, both of which are filled with complete dangers to this republic.

Our people are under the illusion that money from Washington is pure manna. They are selling their birthright as free men, their responsibility in a free man's government, in order to get their supposed gifts from heaven. Also there are those who are impatient with the slow processes of local reform and who conceive that all may be good if the Federal Government would only pass a law and set up a bureau and make an appropriation.

Pray do not think that I don't know all of the arguments pro and con. I do. I have been sitting among them for eighteen months. Nor am I arguing at the moment the wisdom or the non-wisdom of these processes. I merely wish to point out this underlying cause of this gigantic growth, and I want to point out one effect which is now being overlooked.

I need not repeat that the original idea of this republic was a Federal Government of limited powers, with the major protection of personal liberties of the citizen to rest upon the states and local government. The Founding Fathers seemed to have a notion that a bureaucrat might be responsive to the will of the people if his head office was down the street instead of 3,000 miles away in a Pentagon Building. That notion is really worth thinking about again.

Step by step, however, the citizen has surrendered a large part of the control of his life to an increasingly centralized government, and that is where a large part of these 2,000,000 Federal civil service employees are coming from.

I will give you an illustration among several hundred that are available, and, in order not to be too personal and hurt your immediate feelings, I will give you one from 2,000 miles away instead of one within ten blocks of this building.

The Federal Government owns about 150 million acres of land in the West which had little purpose except the grazing of animals. In the course of time, the ranges were overgrazed and a great national resource was in danger. The local governments and the state governments complained bitterly that the Federal Government was not looking after its possessions.

I, being in the White House at that time, made the mild suggestion that the Federal Government would make a gift of the surface rights of these lands to the state governments and they could administer them alongside similar large holdings which they had already received in years gone by from the Federal Government, and we would thus save one out of two administrations.

They refused the idea of this gorgeous gift. They refused because they wanted Federal money for improvement and administration of these lands, and the Federal Government, being a big landowner, of course, felt its obligation, and especially as it was spotted with valuable votes.

But the Government, in the exercise of this duty, proceeded to build up a new bureaucracy directed from Washington and to spend money and to convey guidance to the cattlemen and the sheepmen toward the paths of sweetness and light.

Then that bureau, located in the Department of the Interior, began to exfoliate with constantly new functions which grievously duplicated those of the Department of Agriculture.

At this stage, the problem comes up to the Commission on Organization, and we delivered a solemn judgment that, as the problem wholly concerned agriculture, these functions should be placed in that department and thereby eliminate the complete duplication and waste of public funds.

Then comes a cry from the West. They do not want this. They think perhaps they have more influence with the Department of the Interior than they have with the Department of Agriculture. They offer other arguments.

I am wondering if the real answer occurs to you and to them. The people in the public land states should demand the right to administer their own farms and ranges with their own state and county officials. They should have the courage to undertake their responsibilities. Otherwise, they are contributing one more mite to the surrender of man's most precious possession, the liberty of self-government. And that is only a small atom in the complex that is going on in this Government today. I recommend that you give it thought and consideration. The remedy must come deeper than a Reorganization Commission. Thank you!

The Reform of Government*

Fortune

[May 1949]

OVER many years six Presidents and innumerable congressional committees have struggled to reorganize the
executive branch of our government. They have sought
to eliminate the expensive overlapping, the red tape, the confusion and waste that have multiplied with every new assignment
given to the federal government. They have consistently failed
—stopped by the same stone wall. The hundreds of federal
bureaus and departments are often enthusiastic about reforming
somebody else, but their own functions and jurisdictions always
constitute—in their eyes—an exception.

Moreover, each of these agencies looks to some group in the
country—associations of contractors, conservationists, farmers,
labor, bankers, or what not—that rallies to its support and brings
pressure on the Congress to prevent curtailment or even change
in its particular pet. A mere rumor that our Commission was
considering a method to save a few hundred million dollars
annually by consolidating certain overlapping services brought
an organized drive of as many as 2,000 telegrams to a single
Senator. They were signed before the results of our research
had even been published.

The Commission on Organization of the Executive Branch
of the Government, of which I have the honor to be Chairman,

* Reprinted from the May 1949 issue of *Fortune* by special permission of
the editors; copyright Time, Inc.

146

has been working on this tremendous problem for twenty
months. It took up the work on the unanimous mandate of Congress, and it has attacked it with determination, care, and intelligence. Its report, which is now at length complete, and which
has been submitted to Congress, is composed of twenty-four
parts, with "task force" data attached to each. It has been published by the public printer and can be obtained by any citizen
from that office—and should be read.

With the publication of this document there have come requests from Congress and from citizens all over the land that
something be done to prevent special interests of one kind or
another from blocking reorganization, as in the past. And there
is only one answer to this. The American people must themselves undertake the task of supporting these recommendations,
if they deem them wise. The burden now shifts from the shoul-
ders of the Commission to the citizens themselves, who must
undertake a real and continuing responsibility.

Recently a nonpartisan, nonofficial Citizens Committee for
the Reorganization of the Executive Branch has been organized
under the chairmanship of President Robert L. Johnson of
Temple University in Philadelphia. Its purpose is to keep the
Commission's recommendations before the country and not to
allow them to be forgotten, as such efforts have been in the past.
Nothing could give more emphatic proof that the citizens are
interested than to mention the men and women who, on a mere
preliminary canvass, have joined President Johnson's committee.
They include former Vice Presidents Charles G. Dawes and
John Nance Garner, together with former Supreme Court Justice Owen J. Roberts. They also include former Cabinet members, half from each political party, among whom are James A.
Farley, Charles Francis Adams, Jesse Jones, Harry Woodring,
Charles Edison, Patrick Hurley, Ray Lyman Wilbur. They
include many former Senators, Congressmen, and Governors;
two-score college and university presidents; fifty publishers,
editors, and writers; the leaders of women's organizations, of
farm, professional, business, and labor organizations. Soon

President Johnson will have behind him a thousand leaders of caliber from every community in the country.

If the understanding of the American people is achieved, and the responsibilities accepted, I am confident that the obstacles that have hitherto prevented intelligent reorganization of the executive branch will at long last be overcome. History makes clear that wasteful governments cannot survive. Unless our republic, with the burden it must carry, can conduct its business with more economy and efficiency than is now possible, its government will fail—and with it will go the last hope of the liberties of mankind.

Congress, itself plagued by waste and worn by the drives of pressure groups, unanimously created the present Commission in June, 1947. The act called for a bipartisan body of twelve members, one-third to be selected by the Speaker of the House, one-third by the President of the Senate, and one-third by the President of the U.S. The men selected were experienced in government and they were given a liberal appropriation of $2 millions for research that would get to the bottom of the whole matter once and for all.

The fact that twelve tough-minded individuals of different political and ideological views unanimously agreed upon fifteen of these reports—with a few minor dissents—should in itself indicate how exhaustive has been the determination of facts. Our theory was that there are nine ways to kill a cat and that we ought to agree on some of the nine. All of the twenty-four reports have been voted by the majority of the Commission; the dissents, in most cases, apply only to certain recommendations out of many in a report. Often enough, the dissenting minority was itself split into opposite camps. No vote in the Commission was along party lines.

There will always be a difference of judgment, but my own view is that the country should adopt the majority reports—and the sooner the better. If secondary questions do not work out, they can always be remedied. The pattern is a unity. Any major exceptions would damage or destroy the whole.

GOVERNMENT HOUSEKEEPING

The problem of reorganization falls naturally into two areas: first, the housekeeping questions, and second, the organization of particular agencies and departments.

I do not know of a duller subject on earth than the first group, yet it underlies all other reforms. It includes the problems of accounting, budgeting, personnel, procurement of supplies, allocation of space, and renting space—which apply to *all* the agencies of the government. For instance, few people realize that there should be four kinds of accounts in the government: accounting for the expenditure of appropriations, fiscal accounting of debt and currency, accounting for property, and cost accounting. Yet the first variety is kept, not by the executive arm, where it belongs, but by Congress; the second is kept by the Treasury; and the third and fourth are scarcely kept at all.

We found that the government possesses some $27 billions of personal property, and no one knows how much real property, of which there is no systematic accounting. Moreover, expenditures for capital account are mostly not kept separate from current appropriations. We have proposed an Accountant General in the Treasury, who will install accounts, the systems of which are to be approved by the Comptroller General.

The upcoming budget numbers 1,500,000 words, and deals with sums in a jumble that means less than nothing, even to the intelligent. I doubt that the cost of any particular one of the 1,800 agencies in the government can be determined by anyone short of a professional research accountant. We tested out a few. One example was the Forest Service, budgeted under a heading of $26 millions a year, but as other expenditures for this function were entered in many places, it was really costing more than $43 millions a year. Neither Congress nor the public can form real judgments upon such presentations. We have proposed a revolution that is called a "performance budget," and that can offer opportunity for real judgment.

In personnel, the government employs 2,100,000 civilians and has a turnover of 500,000 per annum. There is little attraction for ambitious youth to stay in government service and, equally, there is little opportunity to get rid of the inefficient. We have proposed drastic reforms as to recruiting, better methods of promotion, simplified severance procedure for the inefficient, and different pay scales in order to make the service attractive as a profession for youth. The importance of all this is summed up succinctly in the fact that the government employs 15,000 different skills. We have sought to free these matters from politics and to decentralize their selection under standards to be set up by Civil Service.

In the procurement of supplies the Congress has added enormously to red tape over a period of years, with the intention of preventing fraud. The unhappy result is that on 1,500,000 items of less than $10 cost, purchased each year, the cost of the red tape for each far exceeds $10. We are proposing great reforms by means of the central purchase of articles for common use, and also by the decentralization of special supplies into the various agencies.

One could go on endlessly about these housekeeping questions, but I may sum them up by estimating that more than $1 billion a year could be saved in this field.

THE DEPARTMENTS

The other segment of the Commission's work was the reform of the departments and the administrations to adapt them to specific missions of major purpose. Here the first step was to clear up the situation around the President. In that area there were two major problems. First, from sixty-five to eighty different bureaus, commissions, departments, agencies, etc. (the exact number depending on the notation used), report *directly* to him. In other words, if each were given one hour a week, their affairs would occupy sixty or eighty hours a week, leaving him no time for the major policies of government. In fact, no one does look after many of these. I think we have reduced them to about twenty.

Another problem in this quarter is the impairment of the

President's authority over these executive agencies by acts of Congress during the last sixty years. There are some thirty-seven agencies whose authority is purportedly direct from Congress. The idea that Congress is the board of directors and the President the executive seems to have been lost somewhere. It is impossible to have responsibility without authority, and the Commission wants responsibility re-established from the office boy up.

In the departments we found the Department of State operating some distance off its true beam. We found the supposed defense consolidation not a consolidation but an added chaos. We found the Department of Commerce no longer the transportation center of the government, as it ought to be. We found the Post Office wrapped in red tape and politics. We found the Labor Department denuded of its proper functions by other departments. We found that the Treasury was engaged in activities unrelated to its primary purpose as our fiscal center. We found that the hospitals and medical services of the government require consolidation to save billions; that the veterans' life insurance has no chance of prompt service under its proposed red tape; that construction activities are scattered in a dozen places instead of being consolidated in one effective public-works center.

I could go on at length. I may, however, conclude by repeating that the Commission's reports have been reduced to about 9,000 words each, on the average. I think that any citizen should be interested in reading them, because, if adopted, they would in my opinion result in an average saving in taxes of about $100 per annum per family. Of course, it is dull reading, without romance or rhetoric. Nevertheless, it should be homework for every family that wishes intelligent government.

There are two things I think everyone should remember. In the first place, these recommendations are, in their major aspects, a fitted pattern. They stand or fall together. To give in at one spot, whatever the political pressures, means, almost inevitably, the collapse of the whole.

Secondly, the reform of our government is, like the Commission itself, a bipartisan matter. It concerns *all* citizens of whatever party. The basic question is the attitude of the citizens. In the conduct of their business affairs Americans are very strict with themselves, to get the best they can for whatever they spend. Government is, of course, different from business; yet this common-sense attitude of demanding efficient management and efficient use of money is entirely applicable to its affairs. Indeed, if our freedom is to be preserved, this attitude is indispensable.

On Reorganization of the Post Office and Civil Service

Statement before the Senate Subcommittee on
Post Office and Civil Service,
Washington, D.C.
[June 30, 1949]

A S YOU are aware, the Commission on Organization of the Executive Branch of the Government made radical recommendations for the reorganization of the Post Office Department. The President within the past few days has sent a special message to the Congress commending the Commission's recommendations. A bill drafted by the Commission (pursuant to instructions of the Committee on Expenditures in the Executive Departments) has been introduced into the Senate, being Senate Bill No. 2062.

The Commission, under the leadership of Mr. George Mead and a Task Force under Mr. Robert Heller, made an exhaustive investigation into the whole structure of the Postal Service. The Commission as a whole gave months of consideration to the problems presented. The Commission's report was unanimous, and was reduced to a few simple but vital recommendations. They cover:

GENERAL ORGANIZATION

The setting up of a Director of Posts (or Deputy Postmaster General) under the Postmaster General, together with an advisory board of citizens under the chairmanship of the Postmaster General.

The abolition of all Senate confirmations except the Postmaster General and the Director of Posts, and the substitution of Civil Service open examinations on merit for all employees—thus taking the Post Office service out of politics.

That the Post Office being a vast business organization, receiving and disbursing vast funds, it should be given the flexibility in budgeting, accounting and audit which Congress has conferred on Government corporations, but that it not be incorporated.

RATES

That the rates of first, second, third and fourth class mail should be fixed by the Congress but that the Postmaster General should be directed to fix all other services, including postcards, at such levels as would cover the cost of the services. This includes such items as money orders, postal notes, special delivery, C.O.D. delivery, etc. It was the view that the latter were services given to special groups and should not be supported, in effect, by general taxation.

I might add that my personal view is that fourth class mail, the parcel post, should be included in these categories as the taxpayers are, in effect, subsidizing a special form of merchandise distribution.

The Commission considered that in second and third class rates, there were elements of education and information which merit some subsidy by the taxpayers.

SUBSIDIES

That where the mails are used to subsidize marine and air services, such subsidies should be separately accounted for and appropriated to the Post Office by the Congress in order to bring them into the open.

SAVINGS

It was estimated by our Task Force and accountants that if these reforms were carried out by fixing of subsidiary rates at cost and administrative changes made possible by the reorganization, the deficit could be reduced by something like $200,000,-000 to $300,000,000 from the present $500,000,000.

Removing Obstacles to Economy and to Competence in Government

Address before the Washington Conference of the Citizens Committee on the Hoover Reports, Shoreham Hotel, Washington, D.C.
[December 12, 1949]

SIX MONTHS have passed since our Commission finished its reports to the Congress on economies and improvements in the Executive Branch.

In the meantime, these recommendations have had a magnificent support by the press and the public. Added to this is the astonishing growth of your Committee of Citizens under the admirable leadership of President Johnson of Temple University.

This has become a crusade for the intelligent reduction of the expense of government. It is a crusade to clear the track for competency. It is a non-partisan crusade. It is a job for citizenship rather than partisanship. The Commission itself represented both political parties. Its work is supported by President Truman and by the leaders from both sides in Congress. Your Citizens Committee embraces our two living and wise former Vice-Presidents and five former Cabinet officers from both the Democratic and Republican side. You include educators, writers, editors, publishers, labor, and farm leaders. You come from every state and Congressional district. You are a mighty host and you are in dead earnest.

It was not the field of our Commission to discuss the merit or demerit of governmental policies. Whatever those functions may be, our purpose is to make them work more economically, more efficiently, and with better service in their contacts with the people.

PROGRESS MADE

You can have confidence that you are succeeding.

The last session of Congress adopted several important recommendations of the Commission and of the President. These measures have already secured large savings. In the Defense Department alone they will soon be at the rate of about $1 billion a year, and Secretary Johnson believes they will amount to fully $2 billions without impairing national defense. And other measures have been enacted into law. We are already clearing the tracks for competence in government.

I am going to make some suggestions as to what we should undertake next. But first, I want to tell you four reasons why this crusade of ours has wider implications than specific reforms.

FIRST

FISCAL AND ECONOMIC SURVIVAL

The first implication relates to our fiscal and economic survival.

During these last six months, the financial situation of our Government has become still more difficult. Federal expenditure of over $43 billions and a deficit of over $5 billions are announced for the present fiscal year. I believe it may be much greater for the next fiscal year. We may be turning two Frankensteins loose in the land. Their terrifying names are "Higher Taxes" and "Inflation." We are interested here in combating them.

When you listen to "billions" over the radio, you no doubt try to size them up in terms of your church contributions. I might remark that the decimal point leads a restless and uneasy life in the Federal Government. Those groups of three ciphers which are separated by commas are moving steadily to the left.

Government spending and taxes must be related to increased per capita production. Therein lies the key of increasing new enterprise, increasing real wages to our workers, increasing real income to our farmers, and an increasing ability to give security to our youth and our aged. Government is a powerful element in this progress. The method and amount of taxes can seriously affect productivity.

Our economists seem to agree that taxation beyond 25 percent of our national income will bring disaster. Possibly your life has been brightened by some economists who dismiss the Federal expenditures as amounting to only 20 percent of the national income, anyway. On that subject, if you add up the actual and prospective annual expenditures of the Federal Government and the local governments, and if you truly compute the national income, you will find this warning red light no longer shines with an intensity of only 20 percent but with considerably over 30 percent. This means far more than 30 percent of the national income. It is a combustion of your savings and your possible standards of living.

Some one remarked that about the time we think we can make ends meet, somebody moves the ends. Despite this, you should not be discouraged in the work we have undertaken. Whatever we can accomplish helps confine the two Frankensteins. And we can ask our people to think it over.

SECOND

EDUCATION IN GOOD GOVERNMENT

Second, another of the wider implications of this crusade is its by-product in public understanding. Millions of American people are receiving a lesson in the fundamentals and methods of good government. We are making some of the people economy-minded.

One of our results has been the setting up of Reorganization

Commissions in 20 states and 10 municipalities for a treatment similar to that of our Commission. We are thus clearing other tracks of obstacles to competence in government.

THIRD

PRESERVATION OF THE AMERICAN EXPERIMENT

Third, in a larger sense, this is a crusade to make democracy work. There is today much apprehension lest the American experiment will fail. We have need to re-establish faith that the whole of the Preamble to the Declaration of Independence and the Gettysburg Address are still related to government. If the Republic is not to be overwhelmed, the people must have such methods and systems as will enable good officials to give them good government.

Success in our crusade will help bring faith instead of cynicism and disillusionment.

FOURTH

HELPING IN THE COLD WAR

Fourth, success in our crusade to reduce cost of government is a necessary condition to winning the cold war. We are fighting this war at frightful cost. The way to win that war is to reduce our wastes, give competence a chance, and defer some government ventures. By these reforms and these self-denials, we can help disappoint Mr. Stalin.

A PROGRAM FOR ACTION

The question before us now is how to further these reforms. Somebody said that wisdom consists not so much in knowing what to do with the ultimate as in knowing what to do next.

Obviously many of these reforms require legislation. Our Congressional leaders requested the Commission staff to draft this legislation. The Budget Bureau is co-operating. Congress is a busy institution, and we cannot expect it to do everything all at once. It has the responsibility to inquire into these proposals, and it has the intricate job of putting them into law as far as they meet with its approval.

Having regard for the burdens of our Congress, it would be well to concentrate on some of the most urgent of these reforms. Some may differ on what this list should be. My own belief is that the following are in the most urgent category:

1. Reorganization of Civil Service—the personnel problem.
2. Reorganization of Budgeting and Accounting.
3. Reorganization of the Post Office.
4. Unification of the Federal hospital services.
5. Unification of water conservation services.
6. Unification of agricultural land services.
7. Unification of transportation services.
8. Relief for the President of the United States.

This is not the whole program but it would do to go on with.

I believe that $2 billions of savings and more efficient service to the public is to be had in these areas alone.

The reports of the Commission are filled with facts in support of these eight reforms. I shall only mention them briefly here.

THE CIVIL SERVICE

Above all things, if we are to have economy and service to the people, the country must have a skilled, nonpolitical Civil Service. And one which will attract and hold the best in the land.

At present Red Tape himself dwells in the Civil Service of 2,200,000 employees. The result is an accumulation of waste and dead wood—and discouragement of good officials. The sword to cut this Gordian knot is to decentralize the engagement and control of these employees (except for certain general services) into the departments and agencies. This must be done under rules to be established by the Civil Service Commission and enforced by it.

BUDGETING AND ACCOUNTING

Next on our list of priorities comes Budgeting and Accounting. I am sure you will agree with me that this is one of the dullest subjects on earth, but it is potent nevertheless. The ghost of Alexander Hamilton still wanders in our fiscal machinery. I doubt whether more than 15 men in the world can make head or tail of the 10 million words and sums in the present Federal Budget—certainly not all at one time.

We urge that the Budget be rebuilt on a functional or performance basis, by which the costs of a given function can be compared year by year. That is both before and after taking. This system has been written into the law as to the Armed Services. It should be made universal. Hitherto no one could know what it costs to operate a hospital or the forests. You would need a sort of Geiger Counter to discover it in two dozen different appropriations.

The accounts, except for Government corporations, are kept by the Congress not by the executive agencies. Any executive needs to sit on top of his accounts.

There has been no adequate personal or real property accounting at all. We estimate that the Government has $27 billions of personal property. When officials know more about what all this property is composed of, and where it is, the departments might live off this fat for quite a while.

THE POST OFFICE

The Post Office is a big business. Our criticism is not directed to its 500,000 employees. They are courteous, helpful, hardworking, and the friends of everybody—the nearest agent of Santa Claus most of us meet. What we object to is the form of organization that is a relic of Ben Franklin plus 160 years of oft-conflicting laws. They cover more than 800 finely printed pages.

We want the Post Office set up as a modern business. We want it taken out of politics.

UNIFICATION OF GOVERNMENT HOSPITALS, PUBLIC HEALTH, AND MEDICAL RESEARCH

Next, we propose a unification of the Government hospitals, health service, medical research and guidance to Government grants-in-aid to civilian hospitals. As an indication of waste, there already existed in Federal hospitals, at the time of our investigation, beds for 225,000 patients and only 155,000 were occupied. Yet Congress had made appropriations for, or authorized, hospitals with 50,000 additional beds despite the fact that 70,000 are empty—at a cost of $1,300,000,000. President Truman canceled out $300 millions of this program, and Congress restored the authority.

But beyond savings, we are striving for something even greater. That is better medical service to our Armed Forces, our veterans, and our seamen. We also want this service set up better to stimulate preventive medicine. We want it not to deprive our civilian population of its doctors.

UNIFICATION OF OUR WATER CONSERVATION SERVICES

Fifth on our list of priorities is the Federal conservation of water resources. At present this function is scattered over many agencies. They employ over 5,000 engineers and about 70,000 other people. They overlap; they have duplicate offices; they compete in procurement of both supplies and skills and jobs to do. A pork-barrel floats in those rivers.

We not alone want to save great sums of money but we want to save water.

UNIFICATION OF FEDERAL LAND MANAGEMENT

The sixth on this preferential list is Federal land management. In continental United States, the Federal Government has about 169 million acres of grazing and forest lands administered by the Department of the Interior. We have about 65 million acres of forests and grazing lands administered by the

Department of Agriculture. In the Western states they compete
with each other and, cheek by jowl, each maintains a staff in almost every county. Millions are being wasted "in them thar
hills."

UNIFICATION OF TRANSPORTATION SERVICES

Seventh in these urgencies is solution of a major problem in
Government services to transportation. Aside from the agencies
regulating transportation rates and services, there are about a
dozen agencies scattered over a dozen different parts of the Government to deal with these matters. We must eliminate their
overlap and waste. We should give the people one central agency
to go to when they seek Government service in these matters.

There is something even more vital. The Federal Government directly or indirectly subsidizes or provides facilities for
aviation, highways, waterways, and overseas shipping. We loan
money to the railroads. They are all an essential part of our national defense. We must have co-ordination of our national policies, aiming at the development of a balanced national transport
system. The troubles of the railroads are a daily exhibit.

RELIEF FOR THE PRESIDENT

Finally, there are some 65 different agencies in the Executive
Branch which report directly to the President. If he gave to each
of them an hour a week for administration, he would have no
time to formulate leadership in the major policies of the Government, or attend an occasional game. By our proposals we can
ultimately reduce these sixty-five agencies by more than one-
half.

Beyond this there is a big confusion of authorities between
bureaus and between the Executive and the Congress. They
form great barnacles on the Ship of State. Under our Constitution, in logic and common sense, there can be only one Chief
Executive officer in our Government, delegating authority ultimately down the line to the office boy. In executive matters

Congress should be content to be the Board of Directors, with agencies of inspection and audit to see that their decisions are properly executed.

OTHER REFORMS

There are many reforms, other than the eight goals I have mentioned. We can furnish them on demand.

OPPOSITION

We have oppositions of course. There are still people who hold to the theory of reduced Government expenses but not to its practice. Your job is to minister to their mental disorders. The best treatment is to persuade them to join in this historic movement toward progress and enduring national security.

IN CONCLUSION

These are not merely statistical assertions nor academic theories. These forces reach into every cottage in the land. They carry with them the future of our youth and of our country.

We must conserve our strength and stop wasting our heritage if we are to survive as a free people.

On the President's 21 Reorganization Plans

Statement to the Press
[May 23, 1950]

THE SCORE from the President's 21 Reorganization Plans just acted upon by the Congress is sixteen passed and five missed. Of the five missed, some were either only in part recommendations of the Commission on Reorganization or varied from the Commission's recommendations. The President has the right and the duty to present his own ideas in these matters and the Congress has the duty to pass on all of them.

Of these 21 Reorganization Plans only one was a major operation—that is the Merchant Marine reorganization. The Commission on Reorganization has recommended eighteen major operations. Four of these major operations have been performed up to date. They are, unification of the Armed Services, creation of the General Services Administration, the State Department reorganization, and now the Merchant Marine reorganization. All together we are making progress.

PART IV

SCIENTIFIC—EDUCATIONAL—SOCIAL

On Feeding Germany

Statement for "Common Cause," at
Request of Christopher Emmet
[April 9, 1948]

THERE can be no decent-minded humane person who does not recoil at the periodic famines in Germany. And every thinking person will realize that maintenance of their working vitality is essential if Europe is to be restored and the American taxpayer relieved of this gigantic burden.

These periodic reductions of the ration during the past two years below the endurance level is not due to any ill will or lack of effort on the part of the Military Government in Germany itself. They arise from lack of Russian co-operation; bad crops; destruction of fertilizer factories; added millions of expellees from adjoining areas; a weak local German government in collecting farm supplies; world food shortages; and the paralysis of bizonal manufacturing industries with the resultant lack of exports with which to buy food for themselves. With the British inability to pay their half share, the whole burden is now thrust upon the United States.

I have recently supported additional Congressional appropriations to raise the rations from the unbelievably low 1,350 calories for the "normal consumer" (2,200 is necessary for public health) and to maintain the extra-meal feeding of some 5,000,000 children now in progress.

The total cost to the American taxpayer of feeding the Germans is now at the rate of $600,000,000 per annum, and even this is probably not enough. Nothing but a change in fundamental policies by the Western Nations, so often recommended by many investigators including myself, will remedy the situation.

On American Overseas Aid

Telegram to Mr. Lee Marshall, National Chairman,
New York City
[July 7, 1948]

New York, New York
July 7, 1948

Mr. Lee Marshall, National Chairman
American Overseas Aid
630 Fifth Avenue
New York, New York

I regret to inform you that it will be impossible for me to attend the luncheon of the American Overseas Aid. It is scarcely necessary for me to affirm the many statements I have already made in furtherance of the work of the Committee.

Beginning in 1941 and continuously, including visits of confirmation to 30 countries in 1946 and 1947, I have constantly repeated that the greatest job of reconstruction was the rehabilitation of children made subnormal by the war. The introduction of this program into Germany and Austria by our Government upon my recommendation is today caring for some 6,000,000 such children and thus freeing the funds of your Committee for aid elsewhere.

Your work under Mr. Pate, formerly of my staff, now reaches several million other children and the assistance in moral and financial support by your Committee has been most helpful.

HERBERT HOOVER

On Belgian-American Foundation Student Exchange

Statement to the Press
[October 12, 1948]

THERE is a great proof of the value of systematic exchange of students and professors and of intellectual materials between our country and other nations. Twenty-eight years ago I established a foundation for that purpose with Belgium from residues of the funds of the Belgian Relief Commission. That foundation has an income of about $100,000 per annum. It has given post-graduate scholarships, has exchanged professors, and has published intellectual material over all these years. Today a majority of the faculties of the Belgian Universities are men who have held such scholarships in American Universities. At one time one-half of the then Belgian Ministry were composed of men who had held these scholarships.

Belgium today is the most unwavering friend of the United States in the world. And our Universities and students have been enriched by the visiting Belgian professors and from the American students in Belgian Universities.

On the Uncommon Man

*Remarks by Telephone from New York City to Wilmington
College, Wilmington, Ohio
[November 11, 1948]*

I AM glad to speak even for a few moments in the encouragement to Wilmington College. Wilmington is not soliciting funds. The reason is that the faculty and students are earning their own keep and building their own buildings with their own hands. Although they ask for no money, the good they are doing deserves help from anyone who has any money to give. The country needs the encouragement of people so distinguished in their reliance on self-help. Those who help themselves ought to be helped.

I believe in the mass production of education of our great universities because I see no other way to meet the enormous demand of two and one-half million youth seeking higher education. But our small colleges do a special job in building morals and character. And character is the most precious asset of our country.

We have heard much in these months about the common man. It is dinned into us that this is the century of the Common Man. The idea seems to be that the common man has come into his own at last.

Thus we have developed a cult of the common man. I have not been able to find any definition of who this common man is. Most American men, and especially women, will fight if called common. Likewise in humility we refer to ourselves as made from common clay, but we get mad when anyone says our feet are made of clay.

However, whoever this political common man is, I want him to have all of the unique benefits of the American way of life, including a full opportunity to rise to leadership. And we must have this uncommon sort of men and women, if we are to have leadership in government, in science, in education, in the professions, and in the home.

Let us remember that the great human advances have not been brought about by mediocre men and women. They were brought about by distinctly uncommon men and women with vital sparks of leadership. Many of these great leaders were, it is true, of humble origin, but that was not their greatness.

It is a curious fact that when we get sick, we want an uncommon doctor; if we have a construction job, we want an uncommon engineer; when we get into war, we dreadfully want an uncommon admiral and an uncommon general. Only when we get into politics are we content with the common man.

Whatever these forces may be, you are striving to become uncommon men and women. And the future of America will be in your hands. Our full hope of recovery in the moral and spiritual world is a wealth of uncommon men and women among our people. It is our educational institutions that must promote and train them.

Therefore, I am for Wilmington College. And I want to congratulate its president, its faculty, and its students on three counts. The first is its revolutionary idea of self-help; the second is that it is a small college; and the third, that from it will flow uncommon men and women—and the nation needs them.

"To Lighten Their Darkness"

Reader's Digest
[*February 1949*]

AFTER seeing human suffering in every form, I believe that there are few personal tragedies which exceed the loss of sight. We tremble instinctively to think of being alone in an endless midnight. Surely there is no man whose heart does not go out to the blind—unless he is himself victim of the darker and more desperate blindness which descends not on the flesh but on the spirit.

The darkness and loneliness of being blind are lessened for thousands of men and women by the Braille edition and the Talking Book edition of the *Reader's Digest*, published by the American Printing House for the Blind through the generosity of the American people. Contributions are needed.

Would you make it possible for one more blind reader to be assured of a free copy of one of these two editions? It would be a good deed to let a little more light into the darkness in this New Year.

The Government Cannot Do It All

*Greater New York Fund's Twelfth Annual Campaign
Dinner, the Waldorf Astoria, New York City
[April 25, 1949]*

I PROPOSE to speak but a moment, and then only on one
phase of your noble work. That is a phase which also concerns every city fund or community chest in the country.
We have a steady expansion of government into welfare
activities. I am not here criticizing the expansion of governmental welfare agencies. They have a place in American life—
provided the cloak of welfare is not used as a disguise for Karl
Marx. But parallel with this expansion, we have stupendous
taxation to support the hot and cold war. That makes it difficult for the citizens to support the voluntary welfare agencies.
It requires more personal sacrifice than ever before.

From all this, many citizens ask themselves: For what reasons
must we continue to support the voluntary agencies? Why not
let the Government do it all?

The first short answer to this question is that you cannot
retire from the voluntary field if you wish our American civilization to survive. The essence of our self-government lies in self-
government outside of political government. Ours is a voluntary society. The fabric of American life is woven around our
tens of thousands of voluntary associations. That is, around our
churches, our professional societies, our women's organizations,
our businesses, our labor and farmers' associations—and not
least, our charitable institutions. That is the very nature of
American life. The inspirations of progress spring from these

voluntary agencies, not from bureaucracy. If these voluntary activities were to be absorbed by government bureaus, this civilization would be over. Something neither free nor noble would take its place. The very purpose of this Fund is to keep voluntary action alive.

The second answer to this question is that it is our privately supported and managed hospitals and educational institutions that establish the standards for similar governmental agencies. It is the voluntary institutions which are the spur to official progress. Without them, our governmental healing and educational agencies will lag and will degenerate. Your sole purpose is support of the private institutions.

The third answer to this question is that morals do not come from government. No government agency can create and sustain a system of morals. You perhaps are not working specifically in the religious field, but your works confirm religious faith and morals. You do support the development of sports in our youth. The ethics of good sportsmanship are second only to religious ethics.

There is a fourth answer. Governments and bureaucracies cannot build character in our youth. With the brutalization which is inevitable from war, revitalized character-building has never been as necessary as it is today. Over half the organizations for which you are appealing are, directly or indirectly, for character-building.

There is a fifth answer. The greatest and, in fact, the only impulse to social progress is the spark of altruism in the individual human being. "And the greatest of these is charity" has been a religious precept from which no civilized people can depart without losing its soul. If governments practice charity, then it is solely because it rises from that spark in the hearts of the people. The day when altruism in the individual dies from lack of opportunity for personal expression, it will die in the government. At best, charity by government must be formal, statistical, and mechanistic. Yours is charity in its real sense—not obligatory but from the heart.

There is a sixth reason. The world is in the grip of a death struggle between the philosophy of Christ and that of Hegel and Marx. The philosophy of Christ is a philosophy of compassion. The outstanding spiritual distinction of our civilization from all others is compassion. With us, it is the noblest expression of man. And those who serve receive in return untold spiritual benefits. The day when we decide that the Government is our brother's keeper, that is the day the personal responsibility for our brother has been lost. If you fail, New York will have lost something that is vital to its material, its moral, and its spiritual welfare.

But a simpler answer than all this lies in the Parable of the Good Samaritan. He did not enter into governmental or philosophic discussion. It is said when he saw the helpless man "he had compassion on him . . . he bound his wounds . . . and took care of him."

That is your mission.

The Institute for the Crippled and Disabled

Remarks at Commencement Exercises
New York City
[June 6, 1949]

Mr. Chairman, Ladies and Gentlemen:

I am glad to have received an invitation to take part in these exercises which again mark over 30 years of public service by this institution.

I have been interested in its work all these years through the devoted service of my friends, Mr. Jeremiah Milbank, Mr. Walter Hope, Mr. Samuel Greer, Mr. Bruce Barton, and your Director, Colonel Smith. Thousands of our citizens have contributed to its support, but I need not say to you that during all this time, these men have organized its financial support and directed its organization. I have been greatly interested in eliminating human and national wastes. Here is a private institution that is serving to do both—and do it in the best way—outside of Government.

That this institution is founded upon scientific research, upon invention, and the best that medical science provides needs no repetition from me.

Nor do I need to review to you the blessings it has brought to thousands of handicapped men and women—not only our injured veterans from two wars, but those from civilian life as well.

Even if one did have all the medical and physical aids—many of which have been inventions of this institution—no single person could, alone and singlehanded, make the greatest and fullest use of them without the training provided here. But greater than training, there is given here the confidence that, despite the handicaps, there is still a real opportunity in the world.

What is important is that thousands, who have come here in despair of their future, have gone forth to renewed lives of usefulness and satisfaction.

This place is an eloquent answer to that great spiritual question: Am I my brother's keeper?

This institution is founded in the realm of the spirit as well as the realm of science. That comes, naturally, from the characters of some of America's great citizens—Jeremiah Milbank and his fellow trustees. And it is because of such men that America has distinction in the world today.

On Inauguration of President J. E. Wallace Sterling

Letter to Board of Trustees,
Stanford University, California
[October 7, 1949]

I WOULD have liked to be present on this great Stanford occasion. It is often a great adventure for any university to choose a new president. And it is one in which the trustees have their major responsibility.

In President Sterling there has been no risk and no choice. Character, understanding, scholarship, administrative ability, and love of youth are all combined in him. Stanford will march ahead to greater things under his leadership as it has done under every one of its Presidents.

Yours faithfully,

HERBERT HOOVER

On The Salvation Army

Luncheon, the Waldorf Astoria, New York City
[December 14, 1949]

NO ONE needs explain The Salvation Army. No one
needs describe its multitude of good works. The main
thing to do is to give them more money to do more
good works. Thereby we appoint them the agent of each of us
for a great human service. And in addition to our money, we
can give encouragement to all its members for their devotion.
We can express our gratitude to them and our confidence in
them.

If the Army is in need of a reference—which they are not—
I will sign any words they may prepare.

My knowledge of them goes back over a long span of years.
I had the good fortune to have the acquaintance, and I might
even say the friendship, of General William Booth, and both
his son and daughter who headed the Army. I have seen the
Army's battalions at work in almost every country of the world.
I have seen them fighting in disasters of flood and famine. I
have seen them giving comfort to our boys behind the front
lines of trenches. I said the first lines, not the second. I have
seen them everywhere in the less dramatic daily toil of helping
the unfortunate, the sinful, and the discouraged.

No matter what our dream of Utopia may be in government,
yet after all, it is the primary business of government to keep
open the channels of opportunity. Government must be im-
personal—it lives on statistics and averages. Statistics cannot
reach into the individual human heart. Governments cannot

regenerate character nor uplift the souls of men and women. Governments cannot seek out the unfortunate and the discouraged and regenerate in each of them the courage and faith which restores the dignity of men and women.

Moreover, no matter how perfect our many private institutions of charity may be, The Salvation Army performs a unique service that no others can so magnificently do.

In their Christ-inspired service, they search the byways for those who have fallen lowest, binding their wounds of body and soul, lifting them back into the stream of useful and Christian life.

The world is today invaded by uncertainty and dread. Yet redemption comes not through the blight of fear but through the light of faith. In that service every lover of humanity respects the Army. Even to witness their devotion invokes a spirit of humbleness to all the rest of us. We must always have The Salvation Army by our side.

On Honoring 1949 Football Coach of the Year

Remarks at Football Coach of the Year Dinner,
New York City
[January 12, 1950]

ASIDE from the pleasure of such an occasion, one reason for my being here tonight is escape into a sanctuary where regimentation, unbalanced budgets, subsidies, income tax, foreign relations, coal strikes, war, and murrain—none of them, not one of them, are on this program.

Also in the old reactionary times—over half a century ago—I had a managerial connection with a football team. That was the year of the first game between Stanford, a new university, and the University of California. We did not have a coach simply because there was not even enough money in the treasury to buy a full assortment of armored equipment, which our team seemed to think they must have. However, as we approached the first Big Game, by pledging our hopes of gate receipts, we were able to persuade an athletic goods house to let us have some nice bright outfits.

We had other troubles that day. We were playing the game in San Francisco at the Haight Street baseball park. We hoped there might be 10,000 people attend—and we had printed that number of tickets. But soon after the gates opened, the tickets were all sold and the fans still continued to come. In those times, we Westerners were still in the blissful period of hard money. We had not yet learned about managed currency. Nor had we heard of the social advancement from a tax on gate receipts.

However, being without tickets we took in hard cash. And our student police escorted each customer from the ticket window to the gate to see that no chiselers got in. The gold and silver piled upon us until it overflowed onto the floors.

Then one of our boys gave free entrance to a housewife from across the street for the loan of a washboiler and some dishpans into which to put our money. The Berkeley manager and I had never seen so much money ever before. Not being satisfied to trust anyone with such a gigantic sum, we sat up until three o'clock in the morning and counted every dime of it. The bank counted it all over again the next morning and found we had $18 more. But the sum was over $25,000. And that brings me to my point: we were now financially able to engage Walter Camp from Yale as coach for the next year. That began his long career on the Pacific Coast. Had your organization been alive at that time, I surmise you would have paid Walter Camp the great tribute you are paying Mr. Charles (Bud) Wilkinson tonight.

One of my other pains at that first game was when the teams came out onto the field to play, the captains demanded to know where the football was! There was none. We had to delay the game a half an hour while we sent downtown to get the vital implement. I credited this error to the U.C. manager—and he credited it to me. But Stanford, to our utter surprise, won the game.

I could even claim more, for I managed the finances of our baseball team. I was demoted to that job after having played shortstop a few times.

For many years, I have served as Chairman of the Boys' Club of America. Here we have 400,000 pavement boys from seven years up. And one of our major purposes is systematic training in sports. Incidentally, their sandlots have produced five major league baseball players.

Now all this too personal an account is to qualify myself as a sports fan and to give more weight to a conclusion. I do not need to mention that sports have become an integral part of our

American civilization. And we may be grateful that so far the advance in social concepts has left them out of governmental regimentation.

Sports are still a free enterprise, and because of the freedom they have risen to a national purpose far more important than even their output of constructive joy. This growth over the years has been possible only because of its own rigid voluntary rules of right and wrong coupled with the training that success depends on team play. Thereby has the high purpose of sportsmanship become second only to religion as a moral influence in our country.

On Responsible Citizenship

Letter to President Alvin C. Eurich, State University
of New York, Albany, New York
[January 23, 1950]

New York, New York
January 23, 1950

President Alvin C. Eurich
State University of New York
Albany 1, New York

My dear President Eurich:

I am indeed sorry I cannot be present at your meeting.

Responsible citizenship is indispensable to self-government by a free people.

For generations we have looked to our colleges and universities to prepare young people for the professions and, in more recent years, to train them for an ever-increasing number of specialized careers. Some of our educational institutions have established courses, departments, and even separate schools to train students for careers in government service.

The need for training in the numerous fields of concern to the federal and to state and local governments is self-evident. If public agencies are to operate effectively and with a minimum of uncertainty and lost motion, they must have competent administrators and personnel who know what they are doing and how to do it.

But important as is specialized training for government service, the education of all of our citizens so that they may have a better understanding of the operations of government and a better knowledge of public issues is equally important. Only with such knowledge can people judge whether their government is good, mediocre or poor, whether statements on questions of concern to all are true, partly true or entirely false and whether promises are possible of achievement and at what cost to them.

Every citizen must be capable of making such decisions wisely and must be keenly conscious of his duty to keep informed about public affairs and to participate in them if our system of self-government is to operate at its best.

The part which the State University of New York can have in the development of responsible citizenship is indeed great.

Yours faithfully,

HERBERT HOOVER

Engineering Society of the Moles

Address, New York City
[February 9, 1950]

I BELONGED to your happy profession before I was thrown onto the slippery streets of public life. But no man loses the love of his profession. That comes inevitably from his education and years of service. I believe it holds more deeply for engineers than any other profession. Especially after they have backslid.

The engineer has certain disadvantages compared to the other professions. His works are out in the open where all men can see them. He cannot deny he did it. The doctors' mistakes are buried in the grave. The voters forget when the politician changes the alphabetical names of his failing projects. The trees and ivy may cover the architects' failures. The lawyers can blame the Judge or the Jury. Unlike the clergyman, the engineer cannot blame his failures on the devil.

Moreover, if his works do not work, he is damned. That is the phantasmagoria that haunts his nights and dogs his days. He comes from the job at the end of the day resolved to calculate it again. He wakes in the night in a cold sweat and puts something on paper that looks silly in the morning. All day he shivers at the bugs which will inevitably appear to jolt its smooth operation. As years go by, people forget what engineer did it, even if they ever knew. Usually, they put some politician's name on it, or they credit it to some fellow who used other people's money with which to do it.

But the engineer himself looks back at the unending stream

of goodness which flows from his successes with satisfactions that few other professions may know. And the verdict of his fellow professionals is all the accolade he wants.

THE ENGINEER IS A POTENT ECONOMIC, SOCIAL, AND POLITICAL FORCE

Most people do not know it, but the engineer is a potent political, economic, and social force. By his applications of the discoveries of science, he is the person who really devitalizes national demons, corrects monopolies, redistributes national wealth, and smooths out the rough spots in the social order.

We as a people have mostly rejected the cloven foot of the personal devil. However, we retain demonology by substituting national demons.

Once kerosene oil was a national demon. No one could win an election unless he reproached the villainies that were in it. Then came the engineer with his electric lamp and retired the oil demon as a public menace.

At another time the canals were the national demons—supposedly sucking the blood from the toil of millions. Then came the engineer and made the railroads. In time the sick canals became the object of pity and owners mostly loaded them off on the Government. That was one of the times the capitalists gladly joined the socialists.

Then for thirty or forty years the railways served as the most lively of the national demons. It was a sin to say kind words about them. To defame them was the sure road to salvation—and election. And the statesmen worked for years to put them under. But long before the statesmen had completed their jobs, the engineer had invented the gas engine and the pipe line. Now the railroads receive pity and solicitude from all. That includes the bloated bondholders.

Then anthracite coal ascended to a short term as the national demon. Before this supposedly grinding monopoly had served for more than half a dozen elections, the engineer had produced a dozen substitutes, and that demon is now in complete anguish.

Then rose the electric power companies to the high place as
the national demon. And they now occupy that hot spot. According to the politician, falling water is manna free from Heaven.
This property of the people is supposedly grabbed and sold to
the people by wicked power corporations. Others cry out against
the ruin of scenery. But the engineer is making trouble along
this front. He has so reduced the fuel consumption for mechani-
cal power that most of the potential manna has been relegated
back to scenery. If you look about you, you will find that the
Government is about the only institution which builds hydro-
electric plants, that being a by-product of water conservation.

There are certain sorceries in these matters also. As this is
an amiable occasion, I will not go further with that subject.

Some segments of mankind have given our public utilities a
demoniac character by a disposition to make undue profits from
selling paper to the innocent as well as services to the needy.
They require restraints from the Government. The mustard
plaster of fact can also contribute to cure these sins. That can be
done if more people would employ more engineers more often.

There have been other national demons including Wall
Street and the bankers. Their fearsome visages have today a
distinct cast of sadness. The Government is now hi-jacking their
job. Some day the engineers will prove that the Government's
financial operations can themselves become demoniac.

But again I am getting off of the track of amiability.

THE ENGINEERS AS ECONOMISTS

We engineers sometimes have bright economic thoughts
where the statesmen are slow on the uptake. Many years ago we
announced, right out loud, that the way to lift the standard of
living was to eliminate waste and otherwise reduce the costs of
production. We said that thereby prices would come down and
the people could buy more and employ more people. We said
that thereby hours could be shortened and wages increased. A
few years later the economists also announced the discovery of
this idea. But, in spite of these reinforcements, it seems at times

that the lawmakers have not yet heard it. At least, they are busy increasing waste and pushing costs up by a variety of devices. However, I will get back on the amiability track again.

CORRECTING THE SOCIAL ORDER

I mentioned that our profession revolutionizes the social order. Did not the Moles by their tunnels and bridges enable millions to escape slums into the countryside? Did not the engineers' perfection of the gas engine and the methods of motor car production bring an unheard-of luxury to the whole people? Did it not contribute to maintain equality of constructive joy among mankind? Did not the engineers develop the gadgets which free the housewife to attend Canasta parties?

IN CONCLUSION

Thus despite all his afflictions and agonies the engineer has great satisfactions. And transcendent over all, he has the fascination of watching a figment of the imagination emerge, through the aid of the sciences, to a plan on paper. Then it moves to realization in stone or metal or energy. Then it brings jobs and homes to men. Then it adds to the necessities and comforts of homes. That is the engineer's high privilege among professions.

In Behalf of Boys' Clubs Week, 1950

Recording for Joe DiMaggio's Weekly Radio Program,
New York City
[March 11, 1950]

THANK YOU, Joe DiMaggio, for your great interest in our Boys' Clubs. The American boy, along with his sister, is our greatest national possession. The 1930 White House Conference which I called to study the health and well-being of the children of the United States formulated the famed Children's Charter. At that time I said if we could have but one generation of properly born, trained, educated, and healthy children, a thousand other problems of government would vanish.

Our Constitution provides each and every one with the inalienable right of Liberty and the Pursuit of Happiness. Now, with a boy, we are not so much concerned at the moment with his liberties as we are with his method of pursuing happiness. He and his gang can hunt for happiness destructively. Our proposal is to channel him into constructive joy, rather than destructive glee.

Somebody will say morals are the job of parents, but the best of parents cannot keep him indoors all the time. In the congested districts of our cities his world in the streets is a distorted and dangerous world, which the parents cannot make or remake. So it becomes a public responsibility. That job hinges around what these boys can do every day between school hours and bedtime, on holidays and on Sundays after church. That is the time and place where delinquency and gangsterism develop.

Ours is a problem of creating a place where these pavement boys can stretch their imaginations, where their bent to play and where their unlimited desire for exercise can be channeled into the realms of sportsmanship. We can divert their loyalties to the gang from fighting it out with fists to the winning of points in a game. We let off their explosive violence without letting them get into the police court. And sportsmanship, next to the Church, is the greatest teacher of morals.

Also, ours is a problem of creating a place in which their curiosity as to what makes the wheels of the world go 'round may be turned into finding their natural bent for future life. All which makes the boy a citizen and not a gangster.

That is why, 14 years ago, I accepted the responsibility of becoming the Chairman of the Boys' Clubs of America.

We have over 300 clubs in our 180 cities, with 350,000 boys from 7 to 17. Public-spirited men and women have contributed over $25,000,000 to build these institutions. It costs millions each year to support them.

March 20 to March 26 will be celebrated as National Boys' Club Week. At that time all America will salute the civic-minded men and women who give freely of their time and money to carry on this great work. These men and women deserve the praise and thanks of everyone interested in boys, for these clubs have become one of the greatest character-building institutions in the country outside of the Church.

If there is a Boys' Club in your city—support it. There are a million pavement boys without clubs. If your community is not fortunate enough to have one, contact your civic leaders and find out why your boys are denied the leadership of a Boys' Club.

And I salute you, Joe, as a former member of a Boys' Club and one of the nation's great sportsmen.

Message to The Salvation Army

Kickoff Luncheon, Philadelphia
[April 3, 1950]

SEVERAL months ago when it was my pleasure to address a group of people in New York, I made this observation: "That no matter how perfect our private institutions of charity may be, The Salvation Army performs a unique service that no others can so magnificently do. In their Christ-inspired service, they search the byways for those who have fallen lowest, binding their wounds of body and soul, lifting them back into the stream of useful and Christian life."

These same words seem appropriate for Philadelphia, the city in which the Salvationists held their first meeting in this hemisphere.

I know something of the trying task you have undertaken going from door to door asking friends and neighbors for help. I know something, too, of the disappointments you face—the repeated call-backs you must make—the time and effort you must put in your self-appointed tasks.

It is perhaps an easier task for The Salvation Army than for any other organization, as its appeal is so well known and so compelling. However, I hope resources will flow to you which make this diversion from your great task less consuming of your energies from your real task.

Our brother's care and welfare, instead of being our last concern, should become our first.

I have known The Salvation Army for years, and it was even my good fortune to know General William Booth and his son and daughter, who succeeded him in the leadership of the Army. I have seen the Army's battalions at work in almost every country of the world. Their inspiring Christian spirit, their never ceasing efforts to rescue, to comfort and to rebuild men, women, and children who have been broken in spirit and health has never changed or faltered. Today, perhaps more than at any time in their seventy years of existence, is The Salvation Army needed in this troubled world. We must always have The Salvation Army on our side.

"Pavement Boys"

*Address before the Annual Convention of the
Boys' Clubs of America,
Washington, D.C.
[May 18, 1950]*

WHAT WE ARE DOING

I AM proud that this is my fourteenth year as Chairman of the Boys' Clubs of America. We have doubled in potency in this period. But the real record is that of your President William E. Hall. He entered that office thirty-four years ago and has nursed this effort up from its swaddling clothes. But Mr. Hall and your directors and I are unanimously agreed that the greatest punch and spirit of this national organization comes from your Director, David Armstrong, and his able staff.

The Boys' Clubs of America are a great school. They might even be called the University of the Pavements, for our purpose is mostly directed to the pavement boys in our congested areas.

Here are linked together over 325 institutions with 300,000 to 350,000 boys, with an equipment that $60 millions could not replace and with an annual budget of $7 millions. There were 24 building projects nearly completed in 1949 and 18 more are under way, costing a total of about $5 millions. All these great sums are made possible by generous people who love boys.

If you need some more statistics, I may tell you that there are 35,000 adults giving generously of their time to the Boys' Clubs as boards of directors or auxiliary organizations. The

Clubs are guided by over six thousand trained adult leaders who are the "faculty."

This education includes self-organization and their own discipline in the conduct of their Clubs. It includes testing out their natural bents in shops, crafts, music, and the professions. It includes medical inspection and training in health. It involves every known indoor and outdoor game and sport except horse-racing and golf. It even includes the flying trapeze.

There is no discrimination as to religion or race. Theirs is that equality which is the foundation of free men. The greatest moral training except for religious faith comes from training these boys in teamwork and sportsmanship.

We do not claim that the Boys' Clubs substitute for either Mother or the public schools. We are concerned with the kid from the hour when school is out until he goes to bed or when he gets a holiday. When a boy is inside our doors, Mother has no worry. The police have no worry from some of his primitive instincts.

We have a right to brag a little. We have produced some major league ball players and some great editors and artists. In the last war draft the total number of rejects among our graduates was less than 5 percent as against the national average of over 30 percent. I could tell you of districts where we have reduced delinquency by 75 percent. Over the years we have brought joy into the lives of millions of boys.

You will anticipate my next remark. We need more money and lots of it, for there are 2,000,000 of these pavement boys whom we have not taken care of.

HIS RIGHTS, CHARACTERISTICS, ENVIRONMENT, AND HOPES

The work of the Boys' Clubs is geared to certain ideas.

First. When the Founding Fathers announced the inalienable rights, they laid proper emphasis on the pursuit of happiness. I have no doubt any lawyer would construe that as especially intended to include boys. However, we are not so worried at the moment with his inalienable rights to the pursuit of happiness as we are with his processes in the pursuit.

Second. In pursuit of happiness, the boy has two jobs. One is being a boy and the other is training to be a man.

When the Boys' Clubs contemplate his jobs, we take into account certain characteristics of the animal and his environment. Some years ago I made some observations on these essentials. I have combined them with some further observations to bring you up to date in this important matter.

Together with his sister, the boy is our most precious possession. But he presents not only joys and hopes, but also paradoxes. He strains our nerves, yet he is a complex of cells teeming with affection. He is a periodic nuisance, yet he is a joy forever. He is a part-time incarnation of destruction, yet he radiates sunlight to all the world. He at times gives evidence of being the child of iniquity, yet his idealism can make a great nation. He is filled with curiosity as to every mortal thing. He is an illuminated interrogation point, yet he is the most entertaining animal that is.

The whole world is new to him. He must discover it all over again. All its corners and things must be explored or taken apart. Therefore his should be a life of discovery, of adventure, of great undertakings. He must spend much time in the land of make-believe, if he is to expand his soul. One of the sad things in the world is that he must grow up into the land of taxpayers.

He is endowed with a dynamic energy and an impelling desire to take exercise on all occasions. He is a complete self-starter, and therefore wisdom in dealing with him consists mostly in what to do with him next. His primary instinct is to hunt in a pack and that multiplies his devices. He and his pack can go on the hunt either for good or evil. Our first problem is to find him constructive joy, instead of destructive glee.

To complicate this problem, this civilization has gone and built up great cities. We have increased the number of boys per acre. We have paved all this part of the land with cement and cobblestones. Of these human organisms, perhaps two and a half million must find their outdoor life on these pavements and confined by brick walls. Much of their life is concerned with stairs, light switches, alleys, fire escapes, bells and cobblestones, and a chance to get run over by a truck. Thus these boys are today separated from Mother Earth and all her works, except the weather. In the days before our civilization became so perfectly paved with cement, he matched his wits with the birds, the bees, and the fish. But the outlet of his energies in exploring the streams and the fields is closed to him. The mysteries of the birds and bees and fish are mostly denied to him.

The normal boy is a primitive animal and takes to competition and battle. If he doesn't have much of a chance to contend with nature, and unless he is given something else to do, he is likely to take on contention with a policeman.

I dislike to refer to these boys as "underprivileged." That is only a part-truth. He has better facilities for education and better protection of health than boys in any other country in the world. He suffers less from mumps and measles than his grandfather did; more quickly do we heal his broken bones. He will live longer, and if his start is blighted, the nation will have to board him longer in jail.

He has other gains. The electric light has banished the former curse of all boys, of cleaning lamps and everlastingly carrying them about. The light switch has driven away the goblins that lived in dark corners and under the bed. It clothes drab streets with gaiety and cheer by night. And it is the attraction of these bright lights that increases our problem.

But we are concerned with the privileges which all these bricks and cement have taken away from him. The particular ones with which we are concerned bear on his character and moral stature. This brick and cement foundation of life is a hard soil for his growths. Somebody will say morals are the job of parents. But the best of parents cannot keep him indoors all the time. And the world in the streets is a distorted and dangerous world, which the parents cannot make or unmake. So it becomes a job of public relations.

But there is more than that. The fine qualities of loyalty to the pack are not so good on the pavements. For here the pack turns to the gang, where its superabundant vitality leads it to depredation. And here we make gangsters and feed jails. The way to stop crime is to stop the manufacture of criminals.

This is only a marginal problem to the total boys in the United States. If we can start this marginal group right on the road to character, we will have done more to cure our national ills than either subsidies or so-called security.

And there is more to this than even exercise and morals. There is the job of stretching his vision of life. The right to glimpse into constructive joy, the right to discover an occupation fitted to his inclinations and talents, and the right to develop his personality. The priceless treasure of boyhood is his endless enthusiasm, his high store of idealism, his affections, and his hopes. When we preserve these with character, we have made men. We have made citizens and we have made Americans.

On Award of Approval for Maurice Pate

Letter Read at Presentation of Princeton University
Merit Cup
Princeton, New Jersey
[June 1950]

New York, New York
January 20, 1950

My dear Mr. Stewart:

I do not know anyone in the United States who is more deserving of an award of approval than Maurice Pate.

For more than 30 years, he has devoted his life to the protection and care of subnormal and undernourished children throughout the world. I suppose that he has given service to four million of them and no doubt has saved the lives of a great part of them.

Maurice Pate has many other fine accomplishments. He was an able soldier in World War I and has occupied various positions of trust and responsibility. In every case he has accomplished more than anyone else could have expected from the circumstances with which he was surrounded.

Yours faithfully,

HERBERT HOOVER

Mr. J. Q. Stewart
Princeton University
Princeton, New Jersey

PART V

OUR NATIONAL POLICIES
IN THIS CRISIS

Our National Policies in This Crisis

Broadcast from New York City
[December 20, 1950]

I HAVE received hundreds of requests that I appraise the present situation and give my conclusions as to our national policies.

I speak with a deep sense of responsibility. And I speak tonight under the anxieties of every American for the nation's sons who are fighting and dying on a mission of peace and the honor of our country.

No appraisal of the world situation can be final in an unstable world. However, to find our national path we must constantly re-examine where we have arrived and at times revise our direction.

I do not propose to traverse the disastrous road by which we reached this point.

THE GLOBAL MILITARY SITUATION

We may first survey the global military situation. There is today only one center of aggression on the earth. That is the Communist-controlled Asian-European land mass of 800,000,-000 people. They have probably over 300 trained and equipped combat divisions with over 30,000 tanks, 10,000 tactical planes and further large reserves they can put in action in ninety days. But they are not a great sea power. Their long-range air power is limited. This congerie of over 30 different races will some day go to pieces. But in the meantime they furnish unlimited cannon fodder.

Facing this menace on the Eastern front there are about 100,-

000,000 non-Communist island peoples in Japan, Formosa, the Philippines and Korea. Aside from Korea, which I discuss later, they have probably only 12 effective combat divisions with practically no tanks, air or navy.

Facing this land mass on the South are the Indies and the Middle East of about 600,000,000 non-Communist peoples. There are about 150,000,000 further non-Communist peoples in North Africa and Latin America. Except Turkey and Formosa, these 850,000,000 non-Communist peoples have little military force which they would or could spare.

But they could contribute vital economic and moral strength.

Facing this menace on the Continental European front there are about 160,000,000 further non-Communist peoples who, excluding Spain, have less than 20 combat divisions now available, few tanks and little air or naval force. And their will to defend themselves is feeble and their disunities are manifest.

Of importance in military weight at this moment there is the British Commonwealth of 150,000,000 people, with probably 30 combat divisions under arms, a superior navy, considerable air force and a few tanks.

And there are 150,000,000 people in the United States preparing 3,500,000 men into a gigantic air force and navy, with about 30 equipped combat divisions.

Thus there are 1,300,000,000 non-Communist peoples in the world of whom today only about 320,000,000 have any military potency.

SOME MILITARY CONCLUSIONS

If we weigh these military forces as they stand today we must arrive at certain basic conclusions.

a) We must face the fact that to commit the sparse ground forces of the non-Communist nations into a land war against this Communist land mass would be a war without victory, a war without a successful political terminal.

The Germans failed with a magnificent army of 240 combat divisions and with powerful air and tank forces. That compares with only 60 divisions proposed today for the North Atlantic Pact Nations.

Even were Western Europe armed far beyond any contemplated program, we could never reach Moscow.

Therefore any attempt to make war on the Communist mass by land invasion, through the quicksands of China, India or Western Europe is sheer folly. That would be the graveyard of millions of American boys and would end in the exhaustion of this Gibraltar of Western Civilization.

b) Equally, we Americans alone with sea and air power can so control the Atlantic and Pacific Oceans that there can be no possible invasion of the Western Hemisphere by Communist armies. They can no more reach Washington in force than we can reach Moscow.

c) In this military connection we must realize the fact that the atomic bomb is a far less dominant weapon than it was once thought to be.

d) It is obvious that the United Nations have been defeated in Korea by the aggression of Communist China. There are no available forces in the world to repel them.

Even if we sacrifice more American boys to hold a bridgehead, we know we shall not succeed at the present time in the mission given to us by the 50 members of the United Nations.

OUR ECONOMIC STRENGTH

We may explore our American situation still further. The 150,000,000 American people are already economically strained by government expenditures. It must not be forgotten that we are carrying huge burdens from previous wars including obligations to veterans and $260 billions of bond and currency issues from those wars. In the fiscal year 1952, federal and local expenditures are likely to exceed $90 billions. That is more than our total savings. We must finance huge deficits by further government issues. Inflation is already moving. The dollar has in six months fallen 15 percent or 20 percent in purchasing power. But we might with stern measures avoid the economic disintegration of such a load for a very few years. If we continued long on this road the one center of resistance in the world will collapse in economic disaster.

THE DIPLOMATIC FRONT

We may also appraise the diplomatic front. Our great hope was in the United Nations. We have witnessed the sabotage of its primary purpose of preserving peace. It has been, down to last week, a forum for continuous smear on our honor, our ideals and our purposes.

It did stiffen up against raw aggression last July in Korea. But in its call for that military action, America had to furnish over 90 percent of the foreign forces and suffer over 90 percent of their dead and injured. That effort now comes at least to a measurable military defeat by the aggression of Communist hordes.

Whether or not the United Nations is to have a moral defeat and suffer the collapse of its whole moral stature now depends on whether it has the courage to

(*a*) Declare Communist China an aggressor.

(*b*) Refuse admission of this aggressor to its membership.

(*c*) Demand that each member of the United Nations cease to furnish or transport supplies of any kind to Communist China that can aid in their military operations. Such a course honestly carried out by the non-Communist nations is not economic sanctions nor does it require military actions. But it would constitute a great pressure for rectitude.

(*d*) For once, pass a resolution condemning the infamous lies about the United States.

Any course short of such action is appeasement.

WHAT SHOULD OUR POLICIES BE?

And now I come to where we should go from here.

Two months ago I suggested a tentative alternate policy for the United States. It received a favorable reception from the large majority of our press.

Since then the crisis in the world has become even more acute. It is clear that the United Nations are defeated in Korea. It is also clear that other non-Communist nations did not or could not substantially respond to the U.N. call for arms to Korea. It is clear the U.N. cannot mobilize substantial military forces. It is clear Continental Europe has not in the three years of our aid developed that unity of purpose, and that will power necessary for its own defense. It is clear that our British friends are flirting with appeasement of Communist China. It is clear that the United Nations is in a fog of debate and indecision on whether to appease or not to appease.

In expansion of my proposals of two months ago, I now propose certain principles and action.

First. The foundation of our national policies must be to preserve for the world this Western Hemisphere Gibraltar of Western Civilization.

Second. We can, without any measure of doubt, with our own air and naval forces, hold the Atlantic and Pacific Oceans with one frontier on Britain (if she wishes to co-operate); the other, on Japan, Formosa and the Philippines. We can hold open the sea lanes for our supplies.

And I devoutly hope that a maximum of co-operation can be established between the British Commonwealth and ourselves.

Third. To do this we should arm our air and naval forces to the teeth. We have little need for large armies unless we are going to Europe or China. We should give Japan her independence and aid her in arms to defend herself. We should stiffen the defenses of our Pacific frontier in Formosa and the Philippines. We can protect this island chain by our sea and air power.

Fourth. We could, after initial outlays for more air and navy equipment, greatly reduce our expenditures, balance our budget and free ourselves from the dangers of inflation and economic degeneration.

Fifth. If we toil and sacrifice as the President has so well asked, we can continue aid to the hungry of the world. Out of our productivity, we can give aid to other nations when they have already displayed spirit and strength in defense against

Communism. We have the stern duty to work and sacrifice to do it.

Sixth. We should have none of appeasement. Morally there is no appeasement of Communism. Appeasement contains more dangers than Dunkirks. We want no more Teherans and no more Yaltas. We can retrieve a battle but we cannot retrieve an appeasement. We are grateful that President Truman has denounced such a course.

Seventh. We are not blind to the need to preserve Western Civilization on the Continent of Europe or to our cultural and religious ties to it. But the prime obligation of defense of Western Continental Europe rests upon the nations of Europe. The test is whether they have the spiritual force, the will and acceptance of unity among them by their own volition. America cannot create their spiritual forces; we cannot buy them with money.

You can search all the history of mankind and there is no parallel to the effort and sacrifice we have made to elevate their spirit and to achieve their unity.

To this date it has failed. Their minds are confused with fears and disunities. They exclude Spain, although she has the will and means to fight. They higgle with Germany, although she is their frontier. They vacillate in the belief that they are in little danger and the hope to avoid again being a theatre of war. And Karl Marx has added to their confusions. They still suffer from battle shock. Their highly organized Communist parties are a menace that we must not ignore.

In both World War I and World War II (including West Germany) those nations placed more than 250 trained and equipped combat divisions in the field within sixty days with strong air and naval forces. They have more manpower and more productive capacity today than in either one of those wars. To warrant our further aid they should show they have spiritual strength and unity to avail themselves of their own resources. But it must be far more than pacts, conferences, paper promises and declarations. Today it must express itself in organized and equipped combat divisions of such huge numbers as would erect a sure dam against the red flood. And that before we land another man or another dollar on their shores. Otherwise we shall be inviting another Korea. That would be a calamity to Europe as well as to us.

Our policy in this quarter of the world should be confined to a period of watchful waiting before we take on any commitments.

NATIONAL UNITY

There is a proper urge in all Americans for unity in troubled times. But unless unity is based on right principles and right action it is a vain and dangerous thing.

Honest difference of views and honest debate are not disunity. They are the vital process of policy making among free men.

A right, a specific, an open foreign policy must be formulated which gives confidence in our own security before we can get behind it.

CONCLUSIONS

American eyes should now be opened to these hordes in Asia.

These policies I have suggested would be no isolationism. Indeed they are the opposite. They would avoid rash involvement of our military forces in hopeless campaigns. They do not relieve us of working to our utmost. They would preserve a stronghold of Christian civilization in the world against any peradventure.

With the policies I have outlined, even without Europe, Americans have no reason for hysteria or loss of confidence in our security or our future. And in American security rests the future security of all mankind.

It would be an uneasy peace but we could carry it on with these policies indefinitely even if the Communists should attack our lines on the seas.

We can hope that in time the more than a billion of other non-Communist peoples of the world will rise to their dangers.

We can hope that sometime the evils of Communism and the crumbling of their racial controls will bring their own disintegration. It is a remote consolation, but twice before in world history Asiatic hordes have swept over a large part of the world and their racial dissensions dissolved their empires.

Our people have braved difficult and distressing situations in these three centuries we have been on this continent. We have faced our troubles without fear and we have not failed.

We shall not fail in this, even if we have to stand alone. But we need to realize the whole truth and gird ourselves for troubled times. The truth is ugly. We face it with prayer and courage. The Almighty is on our side.

Index

Abundant Life, 19
Accountant General, 149
Accounting, *see* Government, Federal
Adam, 10, 62
Adams, Charles Francis, 147
Advertising Clubs of New York City, address to, 53-54
Aeronautics, Civil Board, 118; National Advisory Committee on, 118
Africa, North, 204; South, 95
Aggression, 74, 76, 95, 98, 101; Communist, 77, 84, 93, 96, 97, 103, 203, 206; in Korea, 76, 95; weapons of, 101, 102
Agriculture, Department of, 28, 117, 144, 162; land services of, 159
Air Force, 94, 96, 126, 133, 154, 204, 205, 207; Chief of Staff, 129; Secretary of, 127
Aircraft, 101, 102; Russian, 96
Albany, New York, 185
Alger, Horatio, 9
Alliance, 67, 98; with Russia, 65, 70, 74, 92; *see also* Atlantic Alliance, North; Atlantic Military Pact
America, 3, 5, 6, 9, 10, 13, 19, 21, 31, 61, 143, 146, 174–76, 184, 197, 198; Communists in, 18, 63; *see also* American system
American Druggist, 50
American Newspaper Publishers Association, address to, 59–67
American Overseas Aid, 169
American Printing House for the Blind, 173
American system, 3, 4, 6, 11, 18, 20, 30, 51, 60, 158, 172, 174
Anti-Trust Act, 60
Appeasement, 65, 71, 92, 207, 208; by United Nations, 76, 206, 207
Armament reduction, 101
Armed services, 125, 126, 130, 132, 160; civilian control, 122, 124, 128, 130, 134; commander-in-chief, 130, 134; medical service, 161; unification, 27, 116, 122, 123, 128, 130, 133–35, 164
Armed Services Committee, House, 128–31, 132–36; Senate, 122–27
Armstrong, David, 195

Army, United States, 116, 124; Chief of Staff, 129; Secretary of, 126, 127
Arts, 54, 196
Asia, 5, 82, 83, 92, 94, 95, 97, 203, 209, 210; north, 93; south, 94, 95, 204; southeast, 79
Associations, voluntary, *see* Organizations
Atheism, 66, 67
Atlantic Alliance, North, 93, 94, 95, 98
Atlantic Charter, 83, 92
Atlantic Military Pact, 66, 83, 103, 205
Atlantic Ocean, 98, 205, 207
Atomic bomb, 66, 93, 102, 205
Atomic Energy Commission, 117
"Austerity" in England, 19
Australia, 95
Austria, 103, 169
Automobiles, 53, 190
"Average Working Citizen," 16, 18
Aviation, 162

B-36, 132, 134
Baldwin, Hanson, 73, 74, 92
Ballot box, 50, 51, 64
Bank, Export-Import, 89; International, for Reconstruction and Development, 88–90
Bankers, 146, 189
Barton, Bruce, 177
Baseball, 183–84, 196
Belgian-American Educational Foundation, 170
Belgian Relief Commission, 170
Bethesda Hospital, 125
Big Government, 107
Blind, the, 173
Booth, General William, 180, 193
Boys' Clubs, 183, 191–92, 195–99
Bradley, General Omar, 84
Britain, 19, 62, 70, 96, 98; and China, 207; dominions of, 89; in Germany, 167; military strength, 204
Brookings Institution, 40
Budget, Hoover, 23, 108; military, 124, 125, 134, 135; "performance," 125, 149, 160; Truman, 23, 26, 108, 149, 160, 161, 207; unbalanced, 23, 31, 55, 90, 182

211